Real interview questions from t

Data Science
Interviews Exposed

Your One Stop Source for
Data Science Job Interviews

Jane You, Iris Wang,
Yanping Huang, Ian Gao,
Feng Cao

davocado.com

Data Science Interviews Exposed

www.davocado.com

Real interview questions from top technology companies

Data Science
Interviews Exposed

Your One Stop Source for
Data Science Job Interviews

www.davocado.com

Data Science Interviews Exposed

www.davocado.com

Data Science Interviews Exposed

COPYRIGHT © 2015 by Davocado LLC. ALL RIGHTS
RESERVED.

ISBN–13: 978-1511977487

ISBN–10: 1511977485

Praise for the Book

"Finally, we have a book on data science career planning,
interviews preparation, and the skill set development.
The book is written with great care and enthusiasm by a
crew of leading data scientists who have been working in
the field for years with extensive hands-on experience.
The technical interview questions provide an overview of
the essential topics in data science, along with a great
selection of in-depth example questions and carefully
prepared solutions. The book demonstrates the technical
requirements for data science positions by specific
examples, and explains the thought process for approaching
some challenging problems. The non-technical introduction
offers a very insightful and informative view of the data
science job market, followed by extremely useful
guidelines on career planning and development. I enjoyed
reading the book and highly recommend it for anyone who is
interested in starting a data science career."

Shuang Yang, Lead Scientist, Twitter

"The whole Internet industry and many others value data more and more these days, executives want to make decisions based on the facts derived from the data. We witnessed a rapidly rising demand for data scientists over the past years. This book is a 'must-have' book for preparing interviews for data scientists. The questions in technical interview section cover most of the required skill sets that are being assessed in the interviews, and the solutions illustrate how to use those skills through real examples. The solutions are 'right to the point' but are also designed to inspire candidates to get their own thoughts. The non-tech section is the key for entry level candidates to improve their business understanding as well as professionalism. What I like most about this book is how it gives an overview of the day-to-day work of data scientists, so people can have an idea whether this is the right position for their career goals. This overview is also very helpful for people with different backgrounds to improve their skills to fit in a particular data science job."

A Quantitative Marketing Manager, Google

About The Authors

We, the Davocado team, are a group of five passionate data science professionals who has been working and growing our career in the golden time of Data science: Jane You, Iris Wang, Yanping Huang, Feng Cao, and Ian Gao. We are from leading technology companies including Facebook, LinkedIn, Google, Amazon and Microsoft, where data science is the ultimate motor that keeps changing the business and the whole world.

Jane You is a machine learning scientist at Amazon.com. She received her PhD in computer science in Purdue University. During her almost 5 years in Amazon.com, she has been doing customer review analysis, product pricing, demand forecasting, image processing, pattern recognition and recommendation systems. She is passionate about identifying business opportunities from data, and always enjoys learning new technologies.

Iris Wang is a data scientist at LinkedIn. She received her degree in University of Michigan, Ann Arbor, studying Mathematics, Economics and Computer Science. She has been performing web analytics as well as consumer (behavior) analytics. Her passion aligns with applying data science to make awesome products.

Yanping Huang received his PhD in machine learning from University of Washington. His research interests include reinforcement learning and neural networks. He worked at Facebook on recommendation systems and he is now working at Google on marketing technologies for creative content. He enjoys building scalable systems that can automatically make data driven decisions.

Feng Cao received his Master's degree in Computer Science in Case Western Reserve University, specializing on machine learning and artificial intelligence. He worked as a software development engineer in Amazon, focusing on building ML systems and developing ML/NLP solutions to improve catalog data quality. He has broad interests in every technical aspect of a software system, from front end to back end. He believes a robust system is the foundation of a successful data product.

Ian Gao is a data scientist at Microsoft. He received his PhD in Computer Science. Ian has experience working on machine learning projects in areas such as natural language processing, information extraction, and text mining. He believes in data science for social good.

We firmly believe in the power and the potential of data science, yet we are also experiencing and witnessing the dire of becoming a qualified data scientist. We aim to reduce information asymmetry on data science landscape, bridge the gap between the demand and supply of data science talents, and help hundreds and thousands of data science candidates to begin and advance their career.

We will constantly provide new information about our book and our service for our readers and community, please visit our website: http://www.davocado.com.

You can also follow us on Facebook, LinkedIn and Twitter for the latest updates and discussions:

Facebook: https://www.facebook.com/davocado

LinkedIn: https://www.linkedin.com/in/davocado

Twitter: https://twitter.com/DavocadoCareer

Contents

Preface

One of the revolutionary changes in technology industries is that data science is defining how business decisions are made and how business is grown. For example, search engine, social networks, e-commerce, mobile applications, network securities and sharing economy companies are all relying on data science technologies as their vital power to survive or succeed among competitions. We have also seen traditional industries being transformed by data science, and this movement has gone viral. Therefore, most modern companies today have been investing heavily to recruit and grow data science talents. Data science has been constantly rated as the hottest job skills and data science jobs are among the best paying jobs and the most promising career. However, the gap between the vast demand of data science professionals and the supply of highly qualified candidates remains huge. And this is just the beginning of the era where data science is changing the world and everyone's life. Our book, *Data Science Interviews Exposed*, is dedicated to bridge this gap.

We, the Davocado team, are a group of five passionate data

science professionals who have been working and growing our career in the golden time of data science. We are from leading technology companies including Facebook, LinkedIn, Microsoft and Amazon, where data science is the ultimate motor that keeps changing the business and the whole world. We firmly believe in the power and the potential of data science, yet we are also experiencing and witnessing the dire of becoming a qualified data scientist. We have sat on both sides of the table – first as interviewees seeking data science jobs then as interviewers. Amidst our own job hunting endeavors and interviews with other candidates, we deeply understand the hiring expectations and the unstructured nature of data science interviews. So we have consulted and educated lots of candidates, helping them understand the job market, preparing them for the technical interview questions, and hand holding them to successfully land their feet in data science. However, we have also seen many highly talented candidates from different backgrounds fail the interview process, due to the lack of guidance on how to speak the language of data science and how to score the interviews. Alas, there is no single book currently in the market that can address those problems. As a group we are indeed very limited to help individuals through one on one consultation. So we feel the urgency to share our knowledge and experience in *Data Science Interviews Exposed*. We aim to help hundreds and thousands of data science candidates to begin and advance their career.

As much as we want to distribute and share our knowledge and experience, this book is meant to be a guide but not a cheat sheet. As someone who seeks a shortcut to secure a data science job without making much effort, you will be disappointed; however, for serious data science candidates, this book will help you develop methodologies and strategies in preparing data science job interviews. After reading this book, you will get a big picture of the current status of job market, what data science professionals do in their daily jobs, and the skill set required for different data science job roles. You will know how to assess your background and position yourself for the right data science career opportunities; you will also know better where and how to best spend your time preparing for the interviews. That insightful information is a gentle but effective introduction to grasp the most relevant terminologies and ecosystem of data science, where all of us have years of professional experience and deep knowledge. Most importantly, we have carefully selected and compiled representative questions and answers from recent, real data science interviews from highly reputable companies in the industries. We designed the introductions, questions and answers not only to provide real interview question examples, but also to inspire the readers to exercise their own thought process as if they were in interviews.

The book is not just another book about data science in general terms. It aims to be the "must-have book" of data science interviews. It systematically maps out four major components you will need to succeed in data science career planning and interviews: an overview of data science field, preparation before interviews, a systematic selection of technical interview questions, and detailed explanations and answers for them. The introduction (Chapter 1) presents an overview to the data science job market and the book organization. All the readers are expected to read this chapter, and then jump to proper chapters that fit their needs. Chapter 2, 3, 4, 5 talk about the preparations before interviews by going through everything about getting a job in data science field, other than the technical interview questions. These chapters will tell you how to understand different job roles and select the ones that suit you the most (Chapter 2), how to prepare yourself with the right experience to meet the job requirement and your career goals (Chapter 3), how to make a good resume and online profiles to impress the HRs and the interviewers (Chapter 4), and how to prepare for the non-technical interviews questions that aims at testing the candidate's soft skills (Chapter 5). These chapters do not involve heavy technical content; hence we hope readers find them informative as well as interesting. We recommend the readers read through them at least once to avoid the obvious interview pitfalls that the new candidates usually fall into. Chapter 6 of the book contains the typical technical interview questions in the data science interviews. All the questions are either real interview questions or adapted from real interview questions. The questions are divided into eight topics: probability theory, statistical inference, dataset manipulation, product metrics and analytics, experiment design, coding, machine learning, and brain teasers. Chapter 7 attaches the solution and thought process for each question in Chapter 6. We hope the readers can grasp the key points behind each of them, hence be able to apply the approaches to other similar questions in real interviews. Note that, some questions, like product metric and experiment design questions, may have more than one valid solutions. We provide hints as well as sample solutions. Meanwhile, readers are highly encouraged to think out of the box and explore alternative solutions.

Today there can be tremendous amount of information available when preparing data science interviews. Combing through the unorganized materials is not only time consuming and ineffective but also sometimes leads to confusion. We felt the same frustration as you do when we prepared for data science interviews. We hope *Data Science Interviews Exposed* is the most stress-free way to jumpstart your data science career. Meanwhile, we are constantly improving our books. So please feel free to send us any feedbacks, suggestions or corrections you may have about this book.

Happy reading! Happy interviewing!

Jane You, Iris Wang,
Yanping Huang, Ian Gao,
Feng Cao

Davocado Team
davocado.career@gmail.com
www.davocado.com

Chapter 1

Introduction

We feel it is important to write this book because there are few books about data science interview, while the demand of data science positions such as data scientist, data analyst, and data engineer has been growing exponentially. Usually data science job candidates come from various academic backgrounds including computer science, statistics, applied mathematics, physics, finance, operation research or engineering. They are either fresh out of school or have worked in other industries. But school or their previous jobs did not necessarily prepare them with the proper skill sets required by the up and coming data science field. What the industry is seeking are those who can provide end-to-end data science solutions including data gathering and storage, data filtering and mining, model learning and analysis, and data visualization and reporting. The mismatch between data science job requirements and the skill sets of the candidates is mainly due to the lack of a systematic curriculum, necessary training and career preparation for entering data science. For example, computer science students might be good at data manipulation but lack enough knowledge of statistical analysis. As a result, we see many talented data science job candidates fail data science job interviews, while companies struggle to hire enough qualified candidates.

We believe, with proper preparation, candidates with solid quantitative backgrounds in, for instance, analytics, statistics, and engineering, are able to become great candidates for data science positions. The *mission* of *Data Science Interviews Exposed* is to help people succeed in data science job interviews. This book provides insights into the data science job market and career development. In addition, it provides a systematic approach to prepare for data science interviews. Finally, it offers a collection of *real* interview questions with detailed solutions.

1.1   The US data science job market

With the rise of the new big data technology, data science has been gaining traction for several years. In nearly every industry, companies hire data science talents and invest in data science to make their business more data-driven. This trend has propelled the data science job market to grow almost at an exponential rate.

Data science jobs have topped the charts, as shown in indeed.com job trends in figure 1.1. There are job openings under various job titles such as Data Scientists, Data Analysts, and Data Engineers. Moreover, this demand has far outpaced the supply of available talents in data science. The McKinsey [1] report estimates that by 2018, the United States alone could face about $140,000$ to $190,000$ job vacancies in data science positions that require deep analytical skills, as well as 1.5 million managers and

---

[1]http://bigdatawg.nist.gov/MGI_big_data_full_report.pdf

Figure 1.1: Job trends for data science and data analytics, from Indeep.com

analysts with the know-how to use the big data analysis to make effective decisions. It means that demand for data science talent will exceed supply by $50 - 60\%$.

Figure 1.1 shows the geographic distribution of data science jobs, such as data analyst, data scientist, data engineer, business analyst, research scientist, and business intelligence (BI) engineer. Figure 1.3 shows the distribution of job titles among the data science job family. This data is based on the job profiles from LinkedIn on 11/05/2014. It shows that the Bay Area (San Francisco, San Jose) has the highest concentration, followed by New

Geographics Distribution of Jobs

Area	Data Analyst	Data Scientist	Data Engineer	Business Analyst	Research Scientist	BI Engineer
San Francisco Bay Area	4401	4182	6556	2887	695	1668
Great Seattle Area	1263	865	1687	992	153	546
Great Boston Area	2651	1261	1925	2149	437	464
Washitong DC Metro Area	3594	1447	2687	2769	177	2839
Great New York Area	5566	2232	2340	4905	154	1111
Great Chicago Area	2490	845	1036	2265	206	529

Figure 1.2: The geographic distribution of data science jobs, based on the job profiles from LinkedIn on 11/05/2014.

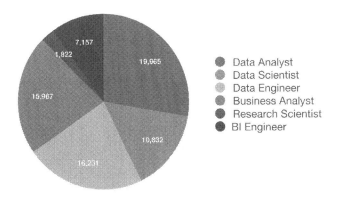

- Data Analyst
- Data Scientist
- Data Engineer
- Business Analyst
- Research Scientist
- BI Engineer

Figure 1.3: The distribution of data science job titles based on survey of the job LinkedIn profiles from five major US cities on 11/05/2014.

York, Boston, Washington DC, Chicago, and Seattle. About 40% are from the Western US, particularly from the high-tech states of California, Colorado and Washington. Within the data science job family, data engineer, data analyst, business analyst, and data scientist are the most popular job titles.

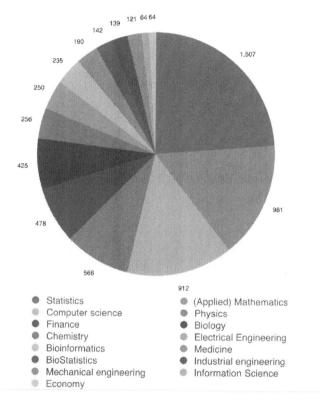

Figure 1.4: The academic background distribution of data scientists in United States. The data is collected from over 5000 data scientists' profiles from LinkedIn on 04/02/2015

Data scientists in the United States come from very diverse academic backgrounds, including computer science, statistics, applied mathematics, physics, finance, and operation research, as shown in table 1.1. Statistics, mathematics and computer science are the top three relevant majors, as most data scientists jobs require statistical knowledge and programming skills. Meanwhile, there are also many data scientists from science, engineering, and business majors. It shows that with proper preparation, everyone from a quantitative background can have a promising career in data science.

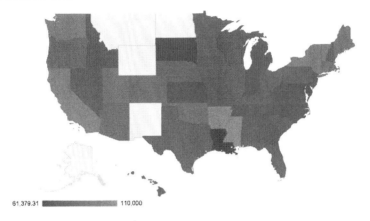

61,379.31 110,000

Figure 1.5: The average salary of foreign workers who got data science related job and in each state, based on disclosure data of foreign labor H1B certification application tables from 2012 – 2015 released by the US Department of Labor.

Data Science jobs are paid very well. A recent survey conducted by O'Reilly Media shows that data scientists' salaries range from $60,000 up towards $130,000, depending on the locations and the degree of expertise using common data science tools. The median data scientist salary in the US is $110,000. These numbers are also backed by the reported median salary, $117,500, for the job title "Data Scientist" from www.glassdoor.com, an employee self-reported salary and job site. Figure 1.5 shows the average salary of foreign workers who got data science jobs and in each state, based on disclosure data of foreign labor H1B certification application tables from 2012 – 2015 released by the US Department of Labor. Additional interactive map visualization[2] is also available.

Keep in mind that for most technology companies, the base salary is only 60%–75% of the total compensation package. There are sign-on bonuses, annual cash bonuses and stock equity. Here are some examples of data scientist compensation packages offered to fresh PhDs:

Sample Compensation Packages

Uber at San Francisco
110k base and 500k worth of Restricted Stock Units (RSU) vested over four years.

Google at Mountain View
127k base with 15% target bonus, a 20k sign-on bonus, and 250 Google Stock Units vested over four years.

Facebook at Menlo Park
130k base with 10% target bonus, a 45k sign-on bonus and relocation fee, and 160k worth of RSU vested over four years.

LinkedIn at Mountain View
128k base with 10% target bonus, and 160K worth of RSU over four years.

Twitter at San Francisco
135k base with a 30k sign-on bonus, and 275k worth of RSU over four years.

Zillow at Seattle

---

[2] www.davocado.com/blog/data-science-job-base-salary-distribution

115k base with a 20k sign-on bonus, a 2k Zillow stock

options

Microsoft at Redmond

110k base with 10% target bonus, a 5k sign-on bonus, and 120k worth of RSU vested over four years.

Amazon at Seattle

105k base with a 25k sign-on bonus for the first year, additional 20k sign-on bonus for the second year, and 250 Amazon stock units vested in four years.

The exact packages may vary depending on background, interview performance, and competing offers. For example, Google and Facebook tend to offer a less competitive package initially, but they are likely to beat the competing offer you have.

1.2   Book organization

In the rest of the book, we will guide you through the process of getting to know the available job positions in the market, finding the proper ones for you, and equipping yourself with interview skills for both non-technical and technical questions. Chapter 2 provides detailed comparisons of different data science jobs ranging from data engineer, data scientist, business intelligence engineer and analyst to data analyst. Chapter 3 talks about different ways of acquiring the right experience to meet the job requirements of your choice. After that, we will show you the tips and tricks on preparing a good resume and online profile to attract HRs' attentions in Chapter 4, followed by instructions on preparing for non-technical interview questions that aim at testing candidates' soft skills in Chapter 5. Finally, in the Chapter 6 and 7 of the book, we present technical interview questions covering frequently asked topics as well as comprehensive explanations to their solutions. All the questions are either real interview questions or adapted from real interview questions. The eight topics we cover are: probability theory, statistical inference, dataset manipulation, product metrics and analytics, experiment design, coding, machine learning, and brain teasers. Readers are encouraged to study the ones that are most relevant to their interested positions, which are described in Chapter 2 and 3, and think out of the box to explore more possibilities than the answers provided in the book.

Let's begin the journey together!

Chapter 2

Find the Right Job Roles

The field of data science is so broad and interdisciplinary that you should understand the various types of job requirements you might be expected to meet. That is, data science positions have a tremendous amount of variations in the functionalities, including data analysis, model building, experiment design, and data reporting. When searching for the right data science position that fits you the most, the key questions you should ask yourself are: what skills do I have and which aspects in data science do I want to focus on?

In addition, in the data science job family, there are lots of different titles, such as data scientist, data analyst, data engineer, business analyst, business intelligence engineer, research scientist, statistician, and business intelligence analyst. These titles sound similar to one another, thus causing confusion to understand the job functionalities behind each title, and to distinguish the differences among them. Candidates may find it very difficult to figure out which positions fit them the best. To clear up the confusion, the following sections will discuss the main functionalities of the four most popular data science roles:

- Data Engineer

- Data Scientist

- Business Intelligence Engineer/Analyst

- Business/Data Analyst

In the following sections, we will provide 2-3 sample job descriptions for each of the aforementioned roles, and show what each particular sample job focuses on and what skills are needed for the job. The reason we analyze those job descriptions is that various job titles have already given great confusion for people who are new to data science; moreover, jobs with the same title within the same company may differ a lot. Thus, understanding the job responsibilities and requirements from the job description is a good skill to have.

To get a further clarification about the role, candidates are strongly encouraged to ask recruiters and hiring managers the detailed information about the role. There are several reasons why the job description might not be specific or accurate. First, it is not uncommon for a company to recycle job descriptions because they are quite generic. Second, job functionalities change during recruiting period but might not be updated on the job description. Thus, if you get a chance to communicate with recruiters and managers, ask them all your questions, and do not make any assumptions. Typical questions to ask include:

- What is the role about?

- What does daily work look like?

2.1 Data Engineer

Being capable of performing data analysis requires having data in the first place. Companies with a large amount of data need to collect, extract, transform and store data in data warehouses in order to facilitate both internal and external customers to do analysis. For instance, Netflix stores the entire user watching histories in order to better understand the correlations between customers and movies, based on which to make better movie recommendations. Uber analyzes real-time supply and demand of private riding in order to automatically adjust surge pricing. All these interesting analytical projects cannot be done without having access to data. The daily work of a data engineer consists of:

- creating and maintaining robust big data pipelines

- performing extract, transform, load (ETL) functions from a data warehouse

- doing data cleaning, conversion, disambiguation and de-duplication.

Generally speaking, data engineer positions prefer candidates to have degrees in computer science, information technology, or related technical fields. However, these types of positions normally do not require a Doctoral degree.

Data engineers' job functionality may differ from company to company, and even from team to team. To get more insights about what data engineers do, let's look at two typical but distinct data engineer job postings.

Data Engineer Case Study One: Facebook [a]

Responsibilities

- Build data expertise and own data quality for the awesome pipelines you build.
- Architect, build and launch new data models that provide intuitive analytics to your customers.
- Design, build and launch extremely efficient & reliable data pipelines to move data (both large and small amounts) to our ridiculously large Data Warehouse.
- Design and develop new systems and tools to enable folks to consume and understand data faster.
- Use your expert coding skills across a number of languages from PHP, Python and JavaScript.
- You have developed applications within the LAMP Stack environment.
- Work across multiple teams in high visibility roles and own the solution end-to-end.

Requirements

- 2+ years of PHP & Python development experience is necessary
- 2+ years of efficient SQL (Oracle, Vertica, Hive, etc) experience is required
- 2+ years of LAMP stack development experience is necessary

- 5+ years of experience with dimensional data modeling & schema design in Data Warehouses

- 5+ years of experience building web applications and expert knowledge of web technologies (HTML/CSS/JS)

- 2+ years of experience in custom or structured (ie. Informatica/-Talend/Pentaho) ETL design, implementation and maintenance

- Unmistakable passion for elegant and intuitive user interfaces

- Experience working with either a Map Reduce or a MPP system on any size/scale

- Ability to write well-abstracted, reusable code components

- Excellent communication skills including the ability to identify and communicate data driven insights

- BS or MS degree in Computer Science or a related technical field

[a]http://tinyurl.com/myekzx3

According to the above post, it is clear that Facebook is seeking data engineers to architect, build and launch data pipelines and data models. This position requires a strong engineering background, with skills in scripting language and knowledge in data modeling and data warehousing. Since this post mentioned mapreduce, it implies that the amount of data to be processed is very large. This position also expects candidates having domain knowledge in web technologies, which implies this data engineer is expected to develop an end to end data product.

Let's take a look at another data engineer job posting from Amazon. These job requirements are different from the first case. Instead of building data pipelines and data models, this one focuses more on "building a platform that can provide ad-hoc analysis to a large dataset". According to the post, it prefers candidates with working knowledge of Oracle BI Enterprise Edition. There may already exist business intelligence solutions, and the job may expect the candidates to maintain and improve current solutions. If there is not yet a business intelligence platform that connects the data sources to end data consumers, it might expect the candidates to design and implement one. We will give more detailed explanations on Business Intelligence Platform when we discuss about the business intelligence engineer in the following section.

Data Engineer Case Study Two: Amazon [a]

Responsibilities:

- Design, implement, and support a platform that can provide ad-hoc access to large datasets.
- Develop interactive dashboards, reports, and analysis templates using Oracle BI EE.
- Model data and metadata for ad hoc and pre-built reporting using Oracle BI EE.
- Interface with business customers, gathering requirements and delivering complete reporting solutions.
- Analyze/Debug existing real time reporting queries and design a unique data model to support real time reporting.
- Tune application and query performance using Unix profiling tools and SQL.
- Significant server side administration duties including maintaining backups, monitoring, application maintenance, and application upgrades.

Qualifications:

- 3+ years' experience with notable BI reporting tool (Oracle BI Enterprise Edition is preferred), including administration, modeling, and development.
- ETL skills (5+ years ETL experience with relational and star schema data modeling concepts).
- Excellent knowledge of Oracle SQL, PL/SQL, Linux and OLAP.
- Oracle PL/SQL performance tuning.
- Server management and administration including basic scripting.
- Basic Oracle DBA tasks.

> **Preferred Qualifications**:
>
> - Bachelor's degree in CS or related technical field and 5+ years experience in Data Warehousing.
> - ETL skills
>
> [a]http://www.amazon.jobs/jobs/289396/data-engineer

The second post does not require the candidate with scripting language skills and web development language skills; it emphasizes the importance of SQL, Unix and ETL (Extract, Transform and Load). It is a process to extract data, transform them into proper format, and load it to a data warehouse or deliver it directly to end-users.

In general, data engineers are the ones to engineer the raw data into proper format so that it can be easily analyzed and stored. Based on the above two examples, it is clear that the focus of the data engineer will vary from company to company, and from job to job. It requires us to read through the detailed job description to figure out whether it is a good fit for you or not.

2.2 Data Scientist

"Data Scientist" has become increasingly popular. People from various majors such as computer science, mathematics, statistics, and physics are lured by this position. What do data scientists do? It is actually a very broad question, since each company, or even each team, has its own definition of data scientist.

In general, the data scientist is the one who dives into data to extract useful information, to assist decision-making, product design, etc. They are impactful in various domains and influence information technology, business, and finance industries heavily. They usually partner up closely with software engineers, data engineers, and product managers. The role involves a great combination of techniques, such as machine learning, data mining, programming, data engineering, predictive analysis, probability models, parallel computing, and data warehousing.

It's rare that a candidate has experience in all the above areas. Different positions focus on a different set of areas. To better understand what is expected by a specific position, it is vital to look into the job descriptions about detailed responsibilities. Even within the same company, data scientists are performing different functionalities in different departments and teams. Take Facebook data scientist positions as an example, if you type "data scientist" in job search box on Facebook career website[1], you will find "Data Scientist, Analytics", "Data Scientist, Product Science", "Data Scientist, Statistics & Decision Science" as well as "Data Scientist, Identity Research & Model". Each position focuses on different problems, and requires different skills. For instance, the job "Data Scientist, Product Science" focuses on difficult problems related to products, while the job "Statistics & Decision Science" focuses more on experiment design and building better statistical tools.

Generally speaking, a good data science candidate should

---

[1]http://tinyurl.com/oqryjj2

possess a set of the following skills:

Curiosity and Passion

You should be passionate about the product and the business of the hiring company, and be curious about how the data can be used to improve it. If you are not self-motivated enough, hardly any skills in the world can help you succeed.

Communication, and presentation

Your soft skills such as team working, inter-personal skills and influencing without authority are as important as your technical skills. For instance, in large organizations, the data you need may come from various sources owned by different teams. And this information might not be fully documented. Having good interpersonal skills enable you to get help in identifying data source and people who might be able to assist. You might need to ask datasource owner to grant you access to data. In addition, you are expected to be able to present the insights obtained from data to your customers in a compelling, accessible manner. What's more, sometimes your conclusions about data are counter-intuitive; you need to be a good storyteller to convince your audience.

Machine learning, data mining

You should be able to make predictive inference from the data. Decision trees, naive Bayesian, logistic regressions, SVMs, neural networks, boosting and bagging are the algorithms and methods data scientists use to get insight from data. You need to find a good learning algorithm that is most suitable for the domain question and select the most relevant features for predictions.

Programming, prototype

You need to know how to work with databases, namely SQL. You should be familiar with at least one of the scripting languages like Python, as well as the associated data processing and statistical computing packages like dataframe, Scikit-learn, and NTLK. You are expected to extract useful data from database, and create a working prototype to demonstrate your models or ideas.

Programming, production

Here you are responsible for not only building the working prototype, but also implementing a robust, reliable, and scalable consumer facing product or service that makes some use of the data. You are expected to figure out how to solve various engineering problems associated with the size of your data set. You also need to write quality code. Otherwise you'll disappoint your fellow engineers in the same production team and cause more work for yourself at the end.

Deep dive data analysis

This is the core of what you can offer as a data scientist. You should be able to define the interesting data needed and select proper tools to collect, process and explore such data in huge volume. You should be able to select the type of analysis to be performed, and implement various algorithms or utilize proper tools to carry out such analysis.

Product insights

You should be familiar with various product related metrics such as engagement/retention rate, ads conversion rate, login session length/count, long term engagement rate, spam rate, and how to measure them.

Experiment design

You should be familiar with the purposes of A/B testing, i.e., seeing whether a new product feature is better or not. As a scientist you also need to know the statistical theory behind A/B testing, how to correctly determine whether the result has statistical significance. You also need to how to randomize users and determine the power of experiment. Last but not least, you are responsible for designing which metrics would be best to optimize, and explaining the experimental results.

Business acumen

The key is to identify the right question and select the most relevant data that can in turn drive business value.

Different data scientist positions expect users to have different combinations of above competencies. In most cases, these positions would prefer candidates to have a master or PhD degree in Mathematics, Computer Science, Statistics, Industrial Engineering, Economics, or other related quantitative and technical fields. In some cases, superb undergraduate students are also considered. Relevant work experience is highly valued in this type of positions. Let's look at some example job postings:

Data Science Case Study One: Amazon HR Analytics [a]

Responsibilities

- Develop analysis plans and implement appropriate statistical techniques to answer complex business questions.
- Independently analyze HR and business outcomes data in order to identify relationships and trends; incorporate data visualization of statistical analyses.

- Develop predictive models for important business- and people-centered outcomes.

- Interact with executive project sponsors across multiple businesses to understand the business outcomes important for success; operationalize those outcomes in ways that can be measured and ultimately predicted.

- Drive the collection of new data and the refinement of existing data sources.

- Interpret data and communicate complex findings to leaders in HR and across business.

Qualifications

- Master's degree in Industrial - Organizational Psychology, Behavioral Economics, Statistics, or related field.

- Strong statistical skills (HLM, regression, ANOVA, IRT methods, Structural Equation Modeling, etc).

- Strong technical skills and proficient in programs such as SPSS, R, Excel, Access.

- You document your approach for reference and reproducibility in the future.

- Self-starter with the ability to work independently.

- Great organizational skills and attention to detail; you are able to prioritize multiple tasks simultaneously without sacrificing the ability to dive deep.

- Ability to communicate complex quantitative analysis in a clear, precise, and actionable manner.

Preferred Qualifications

- PhD strongly preferred in Industrial - Organizational Psychology, Statistics, Behavioral Economics, Statistics, or related field.

- Experience with RedShift and/or Hadoop; preferably with design and deployment.

- Previous work experience in applying statistics to HR and business outcomes.

[a]http://www.amazon.jobs/jobs/281649/data-scientist

This data scientist position is in the Human Resource Analytics team. Due to the unique nature of human resources department, this position welcomes not only candidates with quantitative background, but also candidates from less technical fields, for instance, Industrial-Organizational Psychology, Behavioral Economics, etc. It stresses the importance of statistical background by highlighting some statistical models and tools. It does not mention scalability, which implies that the amounts of data they are working with are not very large. It requires effective, clear, and precise communication skills. This might be a good fit for people with statistics, economics and social science backgrounds.

Data Scientist Case Study Two: Netflix Content Models & Algorithms [a]

Qualifications

- Passion for learning and innovating new methodologies in the intersection of applied math / probability / statistics / computer science. Proficient at translating unstructured business problems into an abstract mathematical framework.

- PhD or MS degree in Statistics, Mathematics, Machine Learning, Operations Research, CS, Econometrics or related field.

- 4+ years relevant experience with a proven track record of leveraging analytics and large amounts of data to drive significant business impact.

- Expertise in predictive analytics/statistical modeling/data mining algorithms. Must have knowledge/experience in some/all of the following: Multivariate Regression, Logistic Regression, Support Vector Machines, Bagging, Boosting, Decision Trees, Lifetime analysis, common clustering algorithms, Optimization, Stochastic Processes.

- Ability to make intelligent approximations of mathematical models in order to make them practical and scalable.

- Proficiency in at least one statistical analysis tool such as R, SAS, and/or Weka.

- Above average capabilities with SQL.

- Experience with distributed databases and query languages like Hive/Pig/Sawzall and/or general map reduce computing is a plus.

- Knowledge of common data structures and ability to write efficient code in at least one language is a plus (preferably Java, C++, Python, or Perl).

- Exceptional interpersonal and communication skills, including the ability to describe the logic and implications of a complex model to all types of business partners.

[a]`https://jobs.netflix.com/jobs.php?id=NFX01074`

This position is dramatically different from the data scientist at Amazon's HR analytics team. Aiming to "satisfy the varied and deeply personal entertainment tastes of our 50+ million members", the job requires candidates to have solid math background, master knowledge of algorithms, and experience with distributed computing environments. From the qualifications, we also see the requirements of deep knowledge in machine learning and data mining. It also prefers the candidate with the capability to write efficient code. Thus, this is a position expecting working knowledge of programming with at least one general purpose language (Java, C++, Python, or Perl), but it might not be a programming intensive position. The coding involved in the job is more likely to be for prototyping, not for production.

Data Scientist Case Study Three: Netflix Product Experimentation [a]

Responsibilities

- Partner closely with Product Management leadership to design and analyze experiments that drive key product decisions.

- Proactively perform data exploration on user behavior to discover future testing opportunities.

- Present your research and insights to all levels of the company, clearly and concisely.

- Research the best metrics to measure user engagement.

- Lead the research and development of new experimentation methods and statistical techniques that could sharpen or speed up decision making.

Qualifications

- PhD or MS degree in Statistics, Mathematics, Operations Research, Econometrics or related field.

- 3+ years relevant experience with a proven track record of leveraging analytics to drive significant business impact.

- Strong statistical knowledge and intuition - ideally utilized in A/B testing.

- Strong SQL skills.

- Experience with distributed databases and query languages like Hive is a plus

- Strong data visualizations skills to convey information and results clearly.

- Proficiency with a statistical analysis tool such as R or SAS.

- Deep product sense.

- Ability to work independently and drive your own projects.

- Exceptional interpersonal and communication skills.

- Impactful presentation skills in front of a large and diverse audience.

- A fan of Netflix is a strong plus

[a]https://jobs.netflix.com/jobs.php?id=NFX02089

This is a great example of data scientist who focuses on product experimentation. This position needs strong knowledge in both product and experiment design. In this scenario, it does not require strong programming skills, neither prototyping or production programming. The coding skill required in this position focuses on extracting relevant data, thus Hive and Pig are desired. It does expect candidates to have strong statistical background, experiment design experience, and deep-dive data analytical skills. In this post, it is specifically mentioned that candidates are expected to have a master or PhD degree, in statistics, mathematics, operations research, econometrics, or related fields.

2.3   Business Intelligence Engineer/Analyst

Business Intelligence engineer (BIE) / analyst (BIA) ranks the 9th best-paying among science, technology, engineering and mathematics (STEM) jobs in 2013, according to Forbes[2].

This position serves the liaison between business and technology. Thus, it expects candidates to have both technical skills as well as business/product sense. Typical Business Intelligence positions focus mainly on two areas, one is data warehousing, the other is reporting.

What is a data warehouse? Imagine this; lots of data are coming in we need a "Mart" or "Warehouse" to store them, so that we can easily and efficiently retrieve them in the future. Data warehouse is the "warehouse" for data. Business intelligence engineers are the masters of the data warehouse. Business intelligence engineers are responsible for loading data from and to data warehouse. Sometime, this process will involve building and set up pipelines; in some cases, data engineers or software engineers will help in this process.

[2]http://tinyurl.com/yu7dqb

Meanwhile, a typical BIE's work also involves creating dashboards for reporting a lot. Reporting involves getting the right data, transforming them into appropriate format, illustrating them with pretty graphs, and sometimes, automating this process. Automating the process of reporting might involve writing scripts. This requires familiarity of SQL and at least one scripting language. In many cases, companies/teams will use business intelligence platforms to automate reporting process. There are a variety of selections of this kind of tools. For instance, Tableau, Oracle OBIEE, Microsoft Power BI, Pentaho, and IBM Cognos. Hands-on experiences with these software products are highly desired.

Communication is also one of the keys to get a position in BIE/BIA as well as long-term career success. On one hand, identifying, collecting, and translating business requirements into actionable items involve heavy amount of communication. On the other hand, extracting insights from large amount of data, presenting key findings and delivering reports also require BIE/BIA to have strong communication skills, so that they can effectively deliver results to various audience with or without technical background.

To further understand Business Intelligence Engineer/Analyst's skill set and job requirement, let's analyze the following two business intelligence jobs:

Business Intelligence Case Study One: Dell [a]

Required Skills

- 6+ years of Data Analysis and SQL skills with a Bachelors degree or 4 years with a Masters degree.
- Demonstrated experience with business intelligence suites, prefer-

ably Pentaho or other open source tools.

- 5+ years of experience with ETL development tools or comparable programming technologies.
- 3+ years of experience leveraging the capability of business intelligence in fast moving small and medium-sized data environments using RDBMS, flat file, and XML data sources.
- 5+ years data modeling - experience in dimensional modeling a plus.
- 5+ years in conducting business analysis for BI and performing related data modeling.
- Knowledge of Linux.

[a]`http://tinyurl.com/pm3dqfe`

The position at Dell requires candidate equipped with some data warehousing skills including ETL development tools. Business intelligence tool is also highlighted; the post explicitly mentions Pentaho, an open source Business Intelligence platform, implying this team prefers their business intelligence tool to be at low cost. In terms of the size of data, the post specifies this is a small and medium-sized data environment, thus currently they haven't faced scalability issues.

This position requires around 5 years of working experience, indicating this is not an entry-level position. However, this does not mean candidates with less experience should not apply. For business intelligence positions, companies generally prefer candidates with more experience, but in most cases they also consider less experienced candidates due to the shortage of talents.

Business Intelligence Case Study Two: Amazon [a]

Responsibilities

- Development of BIE pipeline, including ETL processes which meet business needs.

- Comfortable with creating new business metrics and visual presentation of data with little guidance.
- Rigorous analytical skills to provide insights beyond descriptive statistics.
- Bachelors in statistics, mathematics, operations research, econometrics and 2 to 4 years experience in business intelligence/data engineering roles.
- Highly Proficient with R & SQL.
- Experience with creating Tableau dashboards.
- Comfortable working in a UNIX environment.
- Programming and Scripting experience (Python, Perl).
- Ability to assimilate relevant data sources and hone in on key insights that drive business recommendations.
- Exceptional written and oral communication abilities.
- Master's degree or higher in same fields with 3+ years of experience

[a]http://tinyurl.com/k3vzd7q

This job post from Amazon Studio requires data warehouse knowledge as well. Candidates are expected to create reports and dashboards. In addition, this position expects candidates to have experience with generating new metrics, which stresses the importance of having business senses. Different from Dell's job post, this position demands statistical skills as well as related tools. It also requires programming and scripting language skills, implying this position might involves building data pipeline. This position is undergraduate students friendly – it does not require master or PhD degree.

2.4 Data/Business Analyst

Data analysts wear different hats in different teams and companies. Generally speaking, it expects candidates to be equipped with some of the following skills:

- Strong communication skills. This requirement appears in most data analyst job posts. This type of positions involves heavy amount of communication. In some cases, this individual will become point of contact for internal or external clients.

- Data analytics skills, including familiarity with one or more analysis tool.

- Database and data warehouse knowledge are required for some positions. This skill is needed in companies with large amount of dataset.

- Programming skills. Proficient in SQL and one of scripting language are common requirements in job descriptions. In most cases the candidate is unlikely to be required to write any prototype code, let alone production code. However, it is necessary to know SQL and one scripting language in order to access data in database and perform transformations and statistical computing.

- Reporting, for instance, familiarity with Business Intelligence platform software, for instance, Tableau.

Business analyst positions are very similar to data analyst positions, but normally less technical, having less expectation on programming skills, database and data. Data analyst positions might expect candidates to have knowledge about R or SAS, while business analysts are generally Excel masters.

However business analyst positions do focus more on business sense and the understanding of business process. While both types of positions require strong interpersonal skills, business cannot emphasize more on communications. In some cases, business analysts are also product managers, coordinating different teams working towards the same direction, for instance, improving the product's user experience. In this case, it requires strong project management skills. To be more specific, while there are a lot of different steps in one process, data/business analysts need to step in, gather business requirements, translate vague requirements into actionable items, identify areas of improvement, and look for opportunities, perform cost-benefit analysis, and choose the best options.

The line between business analyst and data analyst can be very blurry in some cases. Thus, we strongly encourage candidates to talk to the hiring manager, or less ideally, the recruiter, about what the daily work of the job position looks like. Since data analyst/business analyst positions vary dramatically, this chapter also lists some job descriptions, and conducts some case studies accordingly.

The below position leans more on the technical side compared to most other data analyst positions. It requires advanced SQL; and specific programming skills are highly preferred. It also expects candidates to perform statistical analysis. This position also requires product management skills as well as strong communication skills in both verbal and written form.

Data/Business Analyst Case Study One: Amazon [a]

Basic Qualifications

- Experience with data analysis, product management, or a similar role.
- Advanced knowledge of SQL.
- Advanced data analysis skills – e.g. Database query construction, data warehousing, pivot tables, experience in market and business analysis.
- Excellent Microsoft Office/PC skills, including strong working knowledge of Excel (Pivot Tables, VLookups).
- Highly organized and results oriented.
- Impeccable attention to detail, passion for processes and systems.
- The ability to work with a wide cross-section of people in various locations.
- Strong written and verbal communication skills.

Preferred Qualifications

- 3+ years of experience in data analysis or data mining.
- Ability to educate others on statistical methods.
- Familiarity with Redshift and/or Tableau.
- Degree in Economics, Mathematics, Statistics, Computer Science or other business/analytical discipline.
- Experience in using statistical software packages, e.g. SPSS, R, MATLAB.
- Advanced experience of Microsoft Excel including Macros.
- Programming skills would be highly advantageous.

[a]http://tinyurl.com/pg9woxc

Generally speaking, this position provides a good opportunity for candidates who come from strong technical and quantitative background, and hopes to move towards a more business-oriented role. Candidates do not necessarily need to have past experience as a product manager to apply for this position. Experiences you gained from side projects or relevant classes also count. Don't wait until you fulfill all the requirements before applying for a job. Most employers understand that candidates are likely to perform really well in some required areas and have some shortcomings. Be honest, and be yourself during the interview. Though you might not have one or some of the required skills, you should show interviewers your strong passions and your desire to learn.

Data/Business Analyst Case Study Two: Microsoft [a]

Responsibilities

- Track and analyze product and business results and drive plans to improve key business metrics.
- Assist in defining Studios strategy and roadmap based on market analysis and internal assumptions.
- Superior analytical and problem solving skills, work with game teams and portfolio management team to manage and track performance to targets and financial plan.
- Work across teams to prepare business and portfolio reviews with insights based on key performance indicators.
- Ability to quickly assess an opportunity's potential, leveraging fact-based analyses and industry experience.
- Personal presence and ability to clearly communicate compelling messages to senior managers and external business partners
- Strong interpersonal and leadership skills to influence and build credibility as a "peer" with Global Functions and Regions
- Team oriented, collaborative, diplomatic, and flexible, with excellent presentation skills, including strong oral and writing capabilities
- Partners closely with business partners to analyze new projects and readiness for governance decisions and provides transparency of portfolio investments.

Qualifications

- Minimum of 5 years of experience in a business analysis role on medium to large-scale projects ideally with experience in the gaming industry.

- Strong leadership, analytical and communication skills coupled with tenacity for taking on initiatives proactively and delivering results.

- Proven track record to deliver independent financial, competitive and global business analysis.

- Can create and present financial statements, business plans, and strategy roadmaps.

- Knowledge of and passion for the games and entertainment industry and the levers that drive hardware, software and services sales.

- Demonstrated history and experience in the games industry developing, measuring and reporting game usage KPIs to establish goals, targets and insights to improve overall game experiences.

- B.A/B.S or equivalent four-year degree.

[a]http://tinyurl.com/pg9woxc

This business analyst position at Microsoft requires much less analytics skills, and much more business sense. In contrast to the previous position at Amazon, this position leans more towards the business side. Reading through this job description, there are no specific requirements on statistical tools and programming skills. This is one strong indicator that this interview tends to focus more on behavior questions, product and metrics problems. In this case, be prepared to discuss all the projects you mentioned on your resume; and be ready for open ended discussions on hypothetical scenarios. Communication skills are vital in this type of position; make sure you talk concisely and clearly.

One important note here is, if you see this type of job description which seems ambiguous, make sure you ask recruiters, interviewers, and your hiring manager:

- What is the most important value this position is expected to bring in into the team?

- What skills are highly valued in this position?

- What does potential daily work look like?

In above sections, we have discussed the differences between major data science job roles. There are a couple of roles not been discussed above, for instance, machine learning scientist and research scientist.

We highly encourage candidates to take close look at job descriptions, and utilize every opportunity to ask recruiters and hiring managers on questions you have. Depending on your interest and specialties, you can identify which job role fits you the best. Once you have a clear idea about what you want to achieve, please refer to next chapter, to find out how to make the dream come true.

Chapter 3

Find the Right Experience

The "right experience" will only come after you fully understand your career goals, your strengths and weaknesses, and the gap between where you are today and where you want to be tomorrow. In this chapter, we help you assess your core competencies to position yourself in the data science field. Then we provide tips and references to help you build up your technical background, skill sets and project experience so that you can have a successful data science candidate profile in your resume.

3.1   Position your career in data science

To get the right experience we suggest you first understand your career interest in data science. What motivates you to get a job in data science? A sense of curiosity by data and passion for analysis? A urgency to find a higher paying job than your current one? Is it the best fit for your statistical or engineering background? Reasons can vary but the more specific answers you have for those questions, the better you can stick with the process of landing a job in data science. It will also help you pick a suitable position from the wide range of job roles in data science.

In previous chapter we discussed four most popular data science jobs. In addition, we strongly encourage you to read the responsibilities of each job description. Usually it is the best place you can get information about the position before you discuss with the human resource (HR) or the hiring manager. We saw many candidates focusing only on the qualifica-
tions and worried about what
qualifications they have or
they do not have. But we
think it is equally important
that the job responsibilities
and the problems the hiring
teams try to solve actually interests you. An interesting job
will keep you happy and moti-
vated, and you will be fulfilled
after 8 to 10 work hours everyday. A happy and interesting job, to a lot of people, is more worthwhile than a well paid but not boring job. Because of this, here we present a few tips to help you better understand whether you would like the day-to-day work of your new job:

- *Assess your personality.*

  Do you like frequent communications with your peers and discussions or do you prefer concentrating on in-depth analysis and building systems?

- *Know people who you will work with.*

  Do you like working with those people and discuss what they are interested in? You can directly ask the hiring manager how many people are in the team, what their job roles are. If you happen to get their names, you can check LinkedIn profiles of co-workers to get a sense of whom you are likely to work with in the new job.

- *Assess your background and strengths.*

  Are you a statistician? Are you a software developer? Are you in a related industry e.g. finance or biostatistics that you want to transit into data science? Although we do think that your future job and career pursuit should highly depend on your interest, we do also want to remind you the common match between the background and the job title in reality:

Typical Job Titles	Typical Background of Employees
Business Analyst	Business or finance background with certain statistics skills
Data Analyst	Strong analytical and data manipulation skills, certain statistical skills or engineering background
Data Engineer	Usually come from an engineering or technical background, with certain experience of data query and scripting skills.
Data Scientist	Normally with advanced mathematical or engineering background, strong algorithm and modeling skills and some engineering skills.

- *Know pros and cons of your new job.*

Usually you want to apply a data science job because it can provide for example the following: a place that can demonstrate your expertise; or they have a data science project you are interested in; or a much better paycheck. Think clearly what you can get out of the new job. At the same time, be aware of the common misperception that the grass is always greener on the other side of the fence. You can find and network with people who are already in those roles and ask them what they like and dislike about their work. After studying the pros and cons you will have a much more realistic picture of your new job and know what you need to do next.

It is common you cannot decide which job role fits you the most. In this case we strongly encourage you to keep multiple job roles in mind and to start to read their qualifications to further prepare yourself for the right experience. Read the basic and preferred qualifications to know which areas you need to improve. Use your best knowledge to assess your fit to those jobs based on your current background and skill sets. Be aware that job descriptions are not necessarily comprehensive. Sometimes hiring managers do not put in a very descriptive summary of the job. They might use a canned version instead. Also keep in mind a job description is usually a piece of advertisement. So the selling point of this job or what the job interests you may only be a small part daily job. *Please read our Chapter 2 where we have done in depth job description analysis and have told you how to know more about the job.*

Case Study

Mr. Smith has a master's degree in statistics and he has been working in an insurance company. He has very good people skills and can easily work with people from various backgrounds. However, he did not have much programming experience since he studied chemistry for his bachelor's degree. He would like to become a data scientist or to hold similar roles in a top tier Internet company, because the pay is higher and the business problems has more impact. He would also like to advance into a management role or a consulting role someday.

In this case we would recommend him looking into business analyst, product analyst or a certain product track of data scientists roles. With good quantitative skills he can be a very strong candidate in product management, sales or marketing management positions. To transit from an individual contributor to a management role, Mr. smith can work on his communication skills, leadership skills and motivational skills. He also needs to expand his vision beyond the problem he solves and grows a sense of what the next business opportunities are, who the customers are and what problems he is going to solve for them. He may start with management experience on smaller projects first.

3.2 General guidance of finding the experience

Once you have studied the qualifications, you can come to the step of identifying what qualifications you meet and what you do not. If you meet most of the jobs' basic qualifications you can skip the following content in this chapter and move on to the next chapter to read about how to polish

your resume and how to prepare for interviews.

If you do find the gap between your current skill sets and
the jobs' required qualifications. We are here to help. In general
we can break down the technical qualifications in the following
aspects:

- *Programming languages.*
  As a data science job candidate, you will be expected to
  have a certain level of programming experience. And some
  job requires fluency in specific languages and libraries

- *Large Scale Data Manipulations.*
  Data query language is almost a must-know for any data
  science job. The most common types are PostgreSQL and
  MySQL that interface with relational databases. If you
  don't know at least one variant SQL then it is really a bum-
  mer in data science job hunting. Because querying transactional databases and pulling data are so fundamental in
  data science that you can hardly get around it. Fortunately,
  SQL is relatively easy to learn. We will introduce some
  good resources in later sections.

- *Algorithms, mathematical models.*
  Algorithm and quantitative models are fundamentals in
  data science. In some extreme cases, we saw companies recruit data science candidates who are strong in algorithms
  and mathematics but only with little programming experience, rather than the other way around. One important
  reason is that tools and software changing all the time, and
  they can be picked up on the job, while algorithms and
  models have more generalized applications. On the other
  hand, algorithms and models are harder to master and
  require some theoretical education background.

- *Visualization and Presentation tools.*
  One thing the data scientist stands out from the other research scientist roles is that it involves a lot of explorative data analysis. And very often data is the evidence of verifying a hypothesis or can assist decision making. Therefore it is critical that you are able to present your data well to justify your hypothesis or to convince people why the decisions can be made based on the data. In other words, you need your data to tell a story. Having the right visualization and presentation is a powerful way to tell people how you interpret your data.

- *Product and business metrics.*
  Rookies in data science may think knowing all models, tools, and libraries is enough for any role in data science. But the ultimate goal of data science is to bring in business insights and to answer business questions. In other words, data science can only be impactful when the results are actionable. So being able to connect your data with the actual product or business problems, is what the majority of hiring managers want to find out in the interview process.

  It is in general difficult to grow your business acumen in a short period of time. Nevertheless we strongly suggest you not overlooking this part when you prepare your interviews for the new job. The most effective way to prepare product and business metrics related questions are reading and reflecting on the job descriptions and responsibilities. It is even better to discuss the job responsibilities with hiring managers if possible. Knowing what the team tries to solve and ask yourself how you would solve it, is a great way of connecting yourself with the business of the new job.

In the following sections, we will explain how to find the experience in each of the aforementioned aspects in more details. We also introduce different learning approaches for candidates who are still in school and candidates who have working experience.

3.3   When you are in school

3.3.1   Data science essentials

If you are currently in school, we suggest you taking mathematics, statistics and computer science courses because those courses are prerequisites to find a data science job.   For mathematics courses, we strongly suggest you taking multivariable calculus and linear algebra. Those mathematical courses will prepare you with comprehensive background knowledge to understand almost all of the probability, statistics and machine learning fundamentals that are required by most of the data science knowledge. For example, multivariate calculus is fundamental in understanding machine learning and probability theory that deal with more than one random variables; linear  algebra is widely used in many model calculations and optimizations in machine learning. After building up solid mathematics background, you can take more courses covering basic probability theory; statistical inference and experimental design, which would further equip you with practical statistics knowledge to do analysis, summary and inference from the observed data.

Essential course studies

- *Multivariate calculus on MIT Open Course Ware* [1].

- *Linear Algebra on MIT Open Course Ware* [2].

- *Matrix on Coursera* [3].

- *Simple and Practical Probability and Statistics* [4].

SQL resources

When preparing programming, you need to learn how to write SQL queries first so that you can extract data from database. As long as the data science job involves reading data from database, you will need SQL sooner or later. Please refer to the following references for learning SQL.

- *W3School SQL tutorail* [5]. It includes almost all basic and common SQL syntax and aggregation functions.

- *SQLZoo* has examples for many advanced SQL functions [6].

- More SQL analytical functions, aggregation functions and ranking functions [7]

Programming languages and libraries

Besides SQL you need to know how to code by learning at least one general-purpose programming language, preferably Python. Python is perfect for data science jobs because of its precise and efficient syntax. In addition, Python also contains nearly all necessary libraries for statistical computing. In data science jobs

---

[1]http://tinyurl.com/pqfvetk
[2]http://tinyurl.com/25xwyd8
[3]https://www.coursera.org/course/matrix
[4]http://tinyurl.com/mwbfb54
[5]http://www.w3schools.com/sql/default.asp
[6]http://sqlzoo.net/wiki/FUNCTIONS
[7]https://msdn.microsoft.com/en-us/library/ms189461.aspx

R and Java libraries and tools are also used depending on the situations. Here we introduce a short list of essentials tools and libraries used by data science jobs:

- *Python* [8] and its IDEs (Integrated Development Environment) such as IPython and Pycharm.

- *Numpy/Scipy* [9], which are extensions to Python to support numeric analysis and scientific computing.

- *Matplotlib* [10], which enables the plotting functionality in Python.

- *Pandas* [11], which offers the data frame and associated data manipulations functions.

- *Scikit-learn* [12], which presents a common interface to many machine learning algorithms.

- *Theano* [13], which provides a great deep learning library and modern GPU computing supports.

- *NLTK*[14], which supports natural language processing and makes text related tasks such as stemming, cleaning and indexing simple and easy.

- *Weka* [15], which provides common machine learning models, friendly data loading and visualization UIs.

- *R* [16] and its IDE RStudio.

---

[8]https://www.python.org/
[9]http://www.scipy.org/scipylib/download.html
[10]http://matplotlib.org/
[11]http://pandas.pydata.org/
[12]http://scikit-learn.org/stable/
[13]http://deeplearning.net/software/theano/
[14]http://www.nltk.org/
[15]http://www.cs.waikato.ac.nz/ml/weka/
[16]http://www.r-project.org/

- *Awk and Sed.* These are powerful scripting languages that can be executed in bash shell albeit they are simple and have existed for a long time.

3.3.2 Data science elective subjects

Here are some elective subjects to help you become a well-rounded data scientist. If you find one of the subjects is particularly interesting, you can also grow a specialization.

- *Machine Learning Books.*

  Machine learning provides tools and algorithms for predictive modeling. Kevin P. Murphy's book "Machine Learning A Probabilistic Perspective" provides a very comprehensive introduction to the field, with demo code and projects that help you better understand the real world applications of machine learning. Christopher Bishop's book "Pattern recognition and machine learning" provides concise and simple explanations of common machine learning models, their mathematics and their intuitions. Stanford Machine Learning course by Professor Andrew Ng on Coursera [17] is also highly recommended.

- *Big Data Technologies.*

  There are tools (Hadoop, Hive, Spark) and frameworks (Amazon Machine Learning, Microsoft Azure Machine Learning) developed specifically to deal with tons of data.

- *Natural Language Processing.*

  Machine learning and statistical analysis only work with structured data, namely, data in the matrix form. However, real data like text are unstructured. It will be a great add-on to your data science arsenal if you learn how to convert

---

[17] https://www.coursera.org/learn/machine-learning

the raw text data into numerical data while still preserving the original "meaning" in the text.

- *Time Series Analysis.*

  This subject helps you make forecasting and understand the underlying dynamics that governs the time series.

- *Product Metrics.*

  You need to develop the business sense to understand what metrics companies track, and how companies measure their success.

- *Optimization.*

  While machine learning helps you formulate the predictive problems as statistical models, it's the optimization that helps you find the numeric solution. Read Stephen P. Boyd and Lieven Vandenberghe's great book "Convex Optimization" if you can.

- *A/B Testing.*

  In most of today's Internet companies, A/B Testing serves as a standard procedure to test which product features work the best. The underlying theory is exactly the same as what pharmaceutical companies have been doing for decades. However, in practice, how to automatically set up A/B testing, how to randomize samples, and how to collect metrics are still challenging projects in most companies.

- *Visualization and reporting.*

  Knowing how to write programs to automatically generate illustrative graphs, plots, and even dashboards you need is a big plus.

3.3.3 Do a capstone project

After taking courses and learning tools, it's time to employ your learned data science and software engineering skills to build some "wow" projects. Another important reason for doing side projects is you can put them into your resume or portfolio. So the projects are better to be clearly defined: it can be a dashboard, a web page, or a new way to understand people's behavior using data, etc.

Here are a few suggestions when you choose your capstone project. If you have just begun to learn data science and only want some basic practice. Kaggle [18]'s "Getting Started" and "Playground Competitions" are great starting points for you to get your hands dirty.

Keep in mind that in Kaggle there are many prize-money competitions. It's tempting to start with those projects. However, those competitions usually have datasets that are too large for the beginners. Moreover, those data sets often require a lot of cleaning and feature engineering. You can easily get lost and get frustrated before you actually implement any predictive models.

Instead of those projects, we recommend you to start with some simple, synthetic, binary classification tasks where you can directly apply some existing machine learning algorithms that

---

[18]https://www.kaggle.com/

Scikit-learn provides. Next, you can play with some slightly more complicated binary classification tasks that contain missing or skewed values and categorical variables. Afterwards, you can try certain multi-class classification tasks or time series regression tasks. Once you are familiar with various types of machine learning tasks, you can find whatever domain that interests you the most and start to work on real data: audio, images, text, etc. Also remember, it's as important to know the limitations of your tools as to know how to use them.

When doing the projects, we suggest you publishing your code in public. For example, create a public Github repository, or publish your solutions/findings via a blog or a post. This would help you connect with other people working on similar projects. And it can be good and concrete data science experience to put on your resume.

3.3.4   Finding an internship

If you have decided to join data science career after graduation, we encourage you to proactively seek internship opportunities in data science. An internship with a reputable company is usually valued more than side projects. You can  usually find internships by campus recruiting events. Or you can express your interest to your advisors and your senior alumni who are working in the data science industry. They will usually have more connections in industry and will be glad to help you out. There are also more and more people using LinkedIn groups to post their interest in finding an internship or a full time job in data science. Believe us, recruiters are monitoring those groups and will reach out to you if you seem to be a good fit. When using LinkedIn profile and groups for your internship, remember to read our Chapter 4 to polish your online profile.

When choosing among different internship opportunities, we encourage you to talk to recruiters or hiring managers, to answer this following question: if you work for this team, can you deliver a valuable project that help you advance in your data science career within 3 months of time? Internship is special because it only lasts for 3 months and in reality many team will use interns to do projects that are not on critical path of the team's success. But we also see quite a few data science internships are doing exciting and experimental projects. So communicate carefully and figure out what you can learn from the 3 months of time.

3.4 When you are from a different industry

We dedicate one section just to discuss the confusions, questions and opportunities for people who want to land a job in data science but previously worked in a different industry. Because data science is so young, only a couple of years old, a lot of data science folks are somewhat transiting from other majors. The most common background you will find among data science people are engineering, computer science, statistics, mathematics, economics, or with experience working with enterprise level data and problem. When you were from a different industry, you also have some working experience. You can use such work experience to your advantage, but you will also need some adjustments and rebranding of yourself.

3.4.1   Programming Experience

For example, many candidates with statistical background use SAS for statistical modeling while a lot of jobs require R language. Essentially SAS and R both have very good libraries for statistical modeling. Python (Numpy/Scipy/Pandas) have powerful toolkit for machine learning and matrix computing. One company's preference of using one than the other is highly dependent on their current systems, their software license policy, whether they have the community support. For example sometimes a language is not chosen due to its in-scalability and the difficulty to integrate with their existing systems.

Not knowing a particular programming language in the job qualification usually will not negatively impact your candidacy in your job. But you will have to know at least one popular programming language and its IDE to do statistical modeling. Please refer to section "Programming languages and libraries" in Chapter "When you are in school" for an essential list of such languages and their IDEs  that are commonly used in data science jobs and companies. The best approach to get experience is by doing a small project using the language. In *When you are in school* we used Kaggle.com as an examplar platform where you can learn by doing real projects.

We have encountered many candidates who primarily programmed in Matlab because it is widely used in academics. It is, however, not very popular in the industry. That is partly due to the fact that candidates who primarily use Matlab are usually from an optimization background or an image processing background. In Internet-based companies, there are not many enterprise level applications that are developed in Matlab. In addition, running Matlab in a profitable company requires a pretty expensive license, therefore candidates who can only program in Matlab will sometimes raise concerns unless he or she has very strong background in other aspects, and there is a risk that he or she will not be considered as a strong candidate.

Candidates with working experience usually know SQL. But over the past decade other types of storage and query system for big data are developed and widely used. DynamoDB and HBase are examples for NoSQL databases. HIVE and PIG are query languages interfacing with Hadoop file system and they can be used to write MapReduce jobs to process large scale data set. Recently there is also Spark which is a more lightweight computing paradigm than Hadoop. Scala, python and even Java 8 functional programming can interface with and run Spark jobs. IPython Notebook is a good start to interface with spark jobs.

Do not panic if you have no knowledge about the data manipulation and query languages other than SQL. From both our experience and feedback from candidates on the job markets; most companies do not test NoSQL knowledge (unless you specify you are familiar with it on your resume). They usually hold the attitude that you can learn on the job. Having a strong SQL skill is convincing evidence that a candidate is capable of picking up other query languages quickly.

3.4.2 Algorithms, mathematical models and experience

In general data science requires at least undergraduate courses study in *linear algebra, numerical optimization, multivariate calculus, statistics and probability*, which can help you to understand more advanced topics such as machine learning. Please refer to section "essential course studies" in Chapter "When you are in school" for a list of resources that can help you quickly ramp up on these topics.

3.4.3   Hard-to-get experience vs. easy-to-get experience

If you are currently working full-time, you will inevitably find adding learning to your busy schedule is difficult. This is why we write this chapter specifically for people who are already working full-time. Compared to students, working professionals who want to ramp up on their data science skills and experience need to work smarter. Before you start to learn new knowledge and skills, you should know what experience is hard to learn and what is easy. For example learning tool set is easy and rewarding. You can get results very quickly and feel like you have achieved something. On the other hand, learning the mathematics and theory behind a model can be time consuming and you may still not understand it. You are not alone. Some of our authors have PhDs in very quantitative disciplines and with years of experiences in data science still find certain models difficult to understand.

Handling small and synthetic data sets are easy to do whereas handling large scale real world data set requires advanced tools and lengthy process of handling noises, missing data and outliers. Knowing what is easy and what is hard can help you to prioritize learning well during your spare time.

Here we share a few tips from the authors through their years of learning and working experience in data science:

- Learning through reading books and materials, especially

learning theory is hard. It will help a lot and prevent you forgetting them if you do exercises after the chapters

- For the same technical content, video lectures and slides are a lot easier to learn. Because video lectures have people explaining details to you and slides have highlighted the most important information.

- When learning a new model, the best way is to use a toolkit and a toy data set to work through an example. For example use scikit-learn to learn a simple clustering algorithm on a data set from UCI Machine Learning Data Sets [19].

- We encourage you to start simple. It is surprising that how a rookie in a domain can overcomplicate things they want to learn.

- We also ask you finishing a project once your start it. This requires you have a predefined scope of your project and simplify the process when you encounter obstacles. For example, when trying clustering and visualizing a data set and algorithm, you may run into "curse of dimensionality", meaning the features you chose are too sparse compare to the amount of data you have. As a consequence all your clusters will be cluttered together. Now it is time you should start to do dimension reduction. However if you don't understand PCA or L1 regression to do dimension reduction, you can resort to some correlation based heuristic feature selection algorithm. This example shows although there are many different way to do feature selections; you can choose a simple one if you don't know a more advanced one.

- Document the (potential) impact and insights of your projects. You can document the motivation, the data analysis discoveries, the metrics you used and the lessons you

---

[19]http://tinyurl.com/ou27uqv

learnt. Keep in mind that the potential impact of the project you did and the insights you gained can be potentially more important than the technical aspect of it. For example clustering algorithms can be simple but using clustering to do customer segmentation is almost being used and explored in every Internet, marketing or consumable companies. Those can be good materials in your resume to impress your hiring managers.

3.4.4   Get the most out of your current job

If now we have already convinced you that you need to do a few projects to fill the gap on the path to your dream data science job, here we try to help you find the resources near you to create such opportunities. Yes, *create* opportunities. We saw many successful professionals and high achievers in career demonstrate very high capability for creating opportunities for both themselves and other people. It is because first it is much easier for you to do your job meanwhile to gain newer experience, rather than moonlighting or doing a side project. The second and a more important reason is, what you did in your job are usually associated with established business metrics therefore have way more impact than your side projects.

However, to get the desired skills for new data science jobs from old jobs you need to proactively exploit your current job. Here are a few tips you can try:

- Talk to your manager (supervisor, advisor etc.), express your interest and seek opportunities. Students will have more freedom to do so, professionals working full time have more difficulties. But keep in mind express why your interest and potential project will bring value to your workplace.

- Find certain mentorship/networking within your company or organization. Experienced professional in data science will give you good advice on what opportunities you can exploit

- Find one project and convince your manager that it will bring value to your org. Below are some options of projects you can consider:
  - Define metrics and build reporting systems to help your organization better define and track success and risks.
  - Build tools, software and processes. And change decision making process to be more data driven
  - Bring in more advanced models and technology to solve existing problems
  - Identify appropriate processes in current business settings (e.g. manual processes) and apply data science to automate the process or reduce operation burdens

- Look elsewhere if your current position definitely cannot provide the experience you want
  - Find a well defined small project to work on. For instance, Kaggle.com hosts data science competition with real datasets. To make your resume look very good, pick interesting problems that have real world values.
  - Find a small group of people who share the same interest with you and are in the same situation. Network-

ing will provides you both motivations and resources. Quora, Meetup, LinkedIn are all good platforms to find peers sharing similar interests.

– Find online courses and even getting a degree in data science. Coursera is one popular choice. It recently opened several data science specializations as well as course works. For instance, University of Illinois at Urbana-Champaign hosts Data Science Specialization, including five course works and one capstone project

– Share your learning with experts and get their feedback. Find someone who is an expert in the area you want to get the experience and ask for his or her guidance and feedback. This will save you tremendous effort and time when learning something new by yourself.

– You can also find professional career development services provider such as Davocado [20], read our book and contact us for advice and counseling.

Now let's go through a case study on how a biometric professional could switch his or her career into data science.

Case Study

Ms. Dubois has a background in electrical engineering. She has been doing biometric research in graduate school, published quite a few papers in fingerprints recognition and got her PhD. After that she got a job as a research scientist in a non-profit bioinformatics institution. Her daily job, not very different from her graduate school years, is reading papers,

---

[20]http://www.davocado.com/

> designing experiments and prototypes, and writing papers. After 1 year and half in the institute, she wants to transit into data science career.

Let's take a close look at Ms. Dubois's background, first we can enumerate what her background matches the required background of a potential jobs in data science.

- Obviously she has quite a bit of pattern recognition and signal processing expertise. She probably used some machine learning models.

- She has certain extent of understanding of probability and statistics.

- She does a certain amount of coding and she can design scientific experiments, know how to choose metrics and how to report results.

- She got years of training in scientific research so she should have independent problem solving capabilities.

Those are what we think the building blocks she can use to step into data science area, she had all the motors and parts. *Purely based on these sets of building blocks, we think she can be a good candidate of data scientist.*

Now let's look at the gap between her background or current job and a data science job in an Internet company:

- The biggest discrepancy here is: she has been working on only a few research topics for so many years, many efforts have gone to improve the specific models she frequently used for her biometric research, e.g. wavelet filters and their variants; But those models may not be applicable to other applications outside of biometrics.

- She has not been using probability and statistical models to model problem on a day to day basis. As mentioned in the previous bullet point, she primarily focused on very specific improvements of a specific model.

- She has not been doing data pulling, manipulation and explorative analysis. Because biometrics data sets used in research institutions are usually small. And she probably has been using the same few data sets as benchmarks for years.

- She has not been coding in Python, Java or SQL that are widely used in an enterprise level software systems and data models.

- Since she mostly works on research topic, it is possible that she has less understanding of business and product metrics; it is also possible that she has less business sense.

Based on the analysis of her profile, we recommend her first use the resources in 3.1 to 3.3 to get some exposure and experiences of skill sets required by data science jobs in most of companies nowadays.

The following two sections are additional information for candidates who want to switch industries and land a job in data science.

3.4.5 Do the homework

Do more research on the industries of your interests, their companies, cultures, pay ranges and ecological systems. For example in internet companies serving general public's interest and consumptions, there are top tier IT companies such as Facebook, Amazon, LinkedIn, Google,

Uber, Airbnb etc.; there are also various data analytical departments are now being established in more traditional

industries e.g. Nordstrom, Home Depot, American Farm Insurance etc.

There are plenty of resources online and an even better way is to find someone in the industries or in the companies to talk to. Or you can also contact Davocado [21] team, we will be happy to help you on these kinds of information and networking.

3.4.6 Profile your strengths and what you can bring in to the new jobs

Many candidates tend to overemphasize the research they have done and the achievements they have on those research. However, future employers are less likely to be interested in what you have done, unless your previous work is gravely related to your future job. What they will all be very interested are what you can bring to the new jobs and evidence that can justify that.

So the candidate should switch to the mentality: *how your qualifications over the years of another domain can bring values to the new job.* Usually those kinds of qualifications come into two types:

- The shared building block of technical qualifications between the old job and the new job

---

[21]http://www.davocado.com/

- Finding new applications for the models or methods in current job. For people who have plenty of business experience, adding business insights and skills to your new job in data science is very much valued.

Chapter 4 of this book will cover more tips on how to highlight your strengths in your resume and online profiles to impress the HRs and the interviewers.

Case Study

Going back to the case of Ms. Dubois, what is common between her current research job and a data science job, is statistics, probability and computing. Also both jobs may include the design of experiments and metrics. So one thing she can brand herself is the solid knowledge and skills of probability and statistics. And she needs to make sure her probability and statistical skills look really solid in the interviews. Ms. Dubois is also an expert of pattern recognition. In a broader sense pattern recognition is an important topic in unsupervised learning. Can she find some such applications where unsupervised learning can play a role in her future jobs? She can also brand her pattern recognition expertise this way.

3.4.7 Present your previous research like a pitch

When we say downplay the previous research you have done, we think you should tread the waters carefully. You will be asked what you have done, although the recruiters might not be interested in the technical details. What they are interested in is whether you could communicate your previous research clearly using layman terms. This is a strong indicator on whether you have insights and big picture of your previous research and whether you are able to communicate complex research ideas to other people. When being asked such questions, do not jump into technical details. Instead, make it an elevator pitch and try to explain your research in 30 seconds with a few sentences? Why are they important and difficult? How did you solve it and what's your contributions? How can you validate your results and quantify the impact? If you can answer those questions well, the recruiters will have the impression that you know what you are doing and you are on top of your work. This impression is way more important than getting them to understand your previous research which probably no more than 10 people in the world can understand.

When you have done all the steps in this chapter and think you are ready for a job for data science, please go ahead and read the following chapter to see how you can condense all your work and qualifications in an effective way and catch the hiring managers' eye.

Chapter 4

Get Ready for the Interviews

Now you have learned about the differences between various data science job roles and how to get the right experience before actually starting to seek a position in data science. In this chapter, we are going to help you earn the entrance ticket for the adventurous journey ahead. The two key things you will need are a good resume and a competitive online professional profile. It will also speed up the process of you getting the interviews if you know how to effectively market yourself to the right positions through internal referrals or by directly contacting recruiters and hiring managers.

4.1   Resume

Recruiters and talent seekers sift through hundreds of, if not even more, resumes every day. They see all kinds of project descriptions, work experiences and even formats. From the resume, they look for the traits of good candidates for the job positions. A good resume can greatly increase your chance to get a job while a carelessly written one will surely make you one of the unfortunate. What are the characteristics that good resumes share? *In fact, good resumes are usually structured, concise, concrete, targeted, and ethical.* The following sections will explain each of these principles in detail.

4.1.1   A well-structured resume draws more eyeballs

You should format your resume so that it is easy for HR to find what they are looking for. Put important information on top and make each section clear. A rule of thumb here is to put skills and work experience before educational backgrounds for experienced candidates, and put educational backgrounds on top for new graduates. You should also consider mentioning your GPA or ranking only if it is really high.

Normally a resume for data science jobs includes the following sections (it may vary depending on different job roles): *Header* (name, email, physical address, phone number), *Skills, Working Experience,* and *Education.* You can optionally add *Project, Re-*

search Experience, Publication, Language, Awards, and *Courses.* For the language, we mean languages like Spanish, Chinese, French, etc. It sometimes helps when the job involves analyzing data in a non-English language, or has a close partnership with foreign companies or branches. In this case, it is a big plus if you happen to know the language.

4.1.2 A concisely written resume is less distractive

Ideally, one page of resume should cover all that is worth mentioning about you. Knowing that a recruiter is reviewing hundreds of resumes on a daily basis means that they are not going to spend more than a couple minutes on your resume. Hence, chances are the second page of your resume will never be carefully looked at. If you think that the contents in the second page will be useful for the interviewers, then you are wrong. Having two pages means that the first page only covers part of you. If you don't want your resume to be rejected because HRs don't see the whole picture of you, then put everything in one page. However, for candidates with more than 10 years experience applying for more senior level positions, 2 pages are considerable.

On the other hand, you are not alone in the group of people who feel they have so many experiences to mention in the resume, that one page does not fit at all. But the truth is, you might not have spent enough time staring at them, evaluating them and thinking about why you put them in the resume. Some people may start the preparation of their resume with writing everything down, and then deleting the least important ones until things fit into one page. It is a good approach to write down everything to make sure that you don't miss anything, unless that it feels bad in the second step where you delete stuff. It is like you are forced to erase parts of your life from your memory, especially the good parts. We understand that your first undergraduate project was a treasured memory for you, but, really, recruiters generally care much less about it when you have a PhD degree.

Here is a better process: write everything down on one piece of paper, grab a second piece of paper, and then with the job objective in mind, start to pull in stuff from the first piece of paper into the second only when it is helpful to qualify you for the job position. This way you don't feel bad because you still have everything in the first paper. *Keep in mind that an entry should not appear in your resume unless there is a good reason to.* Finally, an exception to the one page rule is when you are applying for a scientist role; you probably want to list your publications, which hopefully makes a long list. In this case, having long pages don't hurt. But it is still recommended to put your major achievements in the first page.

4.1.3   Concrete descriptions cover most information

It is better to be concrete when talking about your project experiences and achievements. The point is, if you want to tell people something, demonstrate it in a way so that it can be understood. Otherwise, don't waste your time mentioning it; don't waste HR's time reading it. Something must be important enough to be put in your resume to justify your qualification for the job position. The importance has to be expressed in the resume, concisely but concretely.

There are a few things you can do to make your resume concrete: *using action verb, including quantitative results, clarifying your individual role, and mentioning the key technologies.*

First, using action verbs in the project description emphasizes the achievements you made in each project positively. So try to use verbs like achieved, implemented, improved, etc., and try to avoid simply using verbs like did, worked on, which are plain, hence, less impressive. You can find plenty of lists of good job seeker action verbs online. [1]

Second, including quantitative results is also a good way to highlight your accomplishments. Good examples include but are not limited to mentioning the GPA for your degree, the percentage of performance boost for a certain process due to your work, and the incremental profit you help your company make through your efforts.

Third, clarifying your individual role in a team project is important for the interviewers and HRs to see your leadership and teamwork ability. A bad example can be that you just say you "worked on a project that built an AWESoME robot", where no one really knows what "AWESoME" means, what the robot was capable of and what your real contributions were.

Last but not the least, it is also a good idea to mention the key technologies used in a project to indicate your hands-on experience with them.

---

[1] This is a summary of action verbs from career center at University of Michigan: http://careercenter.umich.edu/article/resume-action-words

4.1.4 A tailored resume for each job position

You should not waste the precious space in your resume and precious HR's time on unrelated things. This is actually aligned with point 2, where we emphasize the importance of the resume being concise. Depending on the specific job position you are applying for, you should tailor your resume to best highlight your qualifications. Note that the time you spent on the resume, which corresponds to how much you value the job opportunity, can be reflected on the contents you put. No one will consider hiring a data analyst who says nothing important but her/his work experience as a bartender, no matter how many more tips she/he earned than other bartenders. Well, unless it is mentioned in the resume that she/he did this by analyzing the customer data and building a model to predict the amount of tip a customer would pay.

A common mistake for people having cross-disciplinary background is to talk too much about their original field, but ignoring to highlight their skills and experiences in the targeted job area. Know that you can *prepare multiple versions of resumes for different job roles*, like financial analyst and data engineer.

4.1.5 Work ethic is the least important, until you miss it

You need to make sure that what you put on your resume is all true, and do NOT lie about yourself. Another common mistake people usually make is to exaggerate about something they don't actually know about. Note that a typical interview usually starts with a conversation about a project on your resume for 10-15 minutes. If you lie about knowing something, which is usually highly related to the job (otherwise you do not need to lie about knowing it), it is very likely you are asked to talk about it. In that case, it is a red flag for the interviewer if your performance doesn't line up with what is stated in your resume, as it shows you have bad work ethic and are not trustworthy.

Just to restate the importance of work ethic, here is a real life example. A candidate who was interviewing for a data scientist position put Hadoop in her skill set on resume. The interviewer, who happened to be interested in this powerful tool for processing big data, started to ask her lots of details about the Hadoop in the interview. Unfortunately, because she did not really have experience working with Hadoop, which she did not want to admit as it was written in her resume, she started to lie about her experience with Hadoop. This obviously did not work, and she ended up failing the interview. Interestingly, after the candidate removed the Hadoop from her resume, she was asked a similar question about Hadoop in another interview for a different position. This time, she frankly admitted that she did not know much about this technology, but was willing to learning it through work. She also told the interviewer that she had hands-on experience with R and successfully impressed the interviewer when being asked about it. She ended up getting the offer. From this example, it is not hard to see how important work ethic is for a candidate.

Although the importance of not making up your experience, you should also know that you do not have to be "proficient" about a technology to mention it in the resume. It does no harm to put job related skills on the resume, as long as you know about them, because it will increase your chance of passing the resume screen.

4.1.6 Miscellaneous

Apart from the aforementioned principles, you also need to pay attention to a few miscellaneous points.

1. A professional resume must neither have any grammar error nor ambiguous information. If you are not a native English speaker, you should consider asking a native friend or career advisor to revise your resume. If you are a student, you should go to the university career center, where there are usually some very professional advisors who can not only polish your resume but also give you useful career advice.

2. Be prepared to talk about the projects on your resume. Know that the first 10-15 minutes of the interview is usually about you talking about your projects and experiences.

3. You should not put any personal information such as age and profile picture on the resume. There is no reason for every rule, for this one, just follow it.

One last trick to draw more attention to your resume is to *include proper keywords about your skill set*. For example, you want to mention the specific technology you used in your project, like Hadoop, Deep Learning, SQL, etc. Due to the large volume of resumes to go through, some companies use a keyword based filtering mechanism to do resume screen. However, the bottomline is that you should not lie about your skill set.

4.2 Online professional profiles

Other than reviewing the resumes that come to them, recruiters also proactively seek good potential candidates through web. One of the biggest platforms for such purpose is LinkedIn.

Some other channels to express yourself to HRs and interviews includes GitHub page, your social network profiles, personal blogs and homepages.

4.2.1 LinkedIn

LinkedIn[2] is a very popular professional network where companies look for potential candidates and job seekers publish their professional profiles. Below are a few tips to help you make most out of your LinkedIn account.

1. **Keep your profile up to date**. You should treat your LinkedIn page like your resume, except that you can always keep it up to date. An up-to-date LinkedIn page shows your investment in online professional presence, which possibly brings potential new opportunities to you and helps people get to know you, thus expands your professional network. HRs apparently know about it, hence they will chase you based on this.

2. **Highlight yourself with proper keywords**. HRs usually search for talents on LinkedIn based on skills or job titles. Therefore, it is very critical that you have the keywords for

---

[2]https://www.linkedin.com

the complete set of skills you possess, and update your job title with brief description of your job responsibilities.

3. **Keep work ethic**. Highlighting yourself with job details does not mean you can expose all the details of your projects. Your profile should not contain any content that is covered by the non-disclosure agreement (NDA) you signed up with your employer. Moreover, you should not put incorrect information about yourself on your profile. Just like what is mentioned in the resume section, you must not lie about your knowledge of certain skills.

4. **Connect with more people**. Social connections and recommendations are effective ways of bridging job candidates with talent seekers. Having a profession LinkedIn account and being connected to professionals will benefit you in the long run by increasing your opportunity of being internally referred to their companies. It will also expand your knowledge about different good companies.

5. **Get endorsement and ask for recommendations**. Earning endorsement and recommendations from your peers or supervisors demonstrates your solid professional skills, as well as social skills. It's a very convincing signal for both recruiters and hiring managers to see that you have made impressive impacts and also are a good team player. A good way to collect endorsements is to first endorse people. They will usually endorse back.

4.2.2 GitHub

GitHub[3] is a web-based project hosting service using Git as version control system. It is becoming more and more popular among engineers to share their side projects, course projects, etc.

---

[3]https://www.github.com

A frequently updated GitHub page will definitely show your hands-on skills and your enthusiasm for product building.

4.2.3 Personal website/homepage

In some cases, there are better platforms than LinkedIn and Github to market yourself. For example, scientists and researchers usually have their own homepage to show their research interests, publications, and project demos. If you fall into this category, it is recommended that you follow the conventions and create an illustrative homepage to showcase your academic background. Even for engineers and data analysts, it is not a bad idea to have a personal website to demonstrate your strengths through customized contents.

Finally, please note that only professional profiles, like the ones we mentioned above, will help you to attract serious talent seekers. Facebook, Twitter, Instagram are social networks that do not reveal your professional skills. Furthermore, they contain too much of your personal information, which is not recommended to be visible by your potential employers.

4.3   Get the right exposure and find the right position

Now that you have a perfectly tailored personal resume and a great-looking professional online profile, what if you still don't get any interviews? Go submit your resume through proper channels.

The most effective channel to get interview is through *employee internal referral*. Ways to find internal referrals include but are not limited to:

1. Ask for internal referrals from your peers who work in

the company you want to join. Since your peers know you personally, they can put recommending words in the referral for you.

2. As for internal referrals from alumni or through social connections. For example you can find the former students of your professor. You can also find your alumni through social networks like LinkedIn. Sometimes, your professor has industry connections and hence can recommend you for a proper position. Don't be shy or embarrassed to ask for referral, as people usually are happy to help get more alumni into the same company, as long as they can find you, or you can find them. Plus they can get referral bonus, which is usually a few thousand dollars, if you eventually join the company. On the other hand they do not lose anything if you fail the interview or reject the offer.

3. Contact HRs directly. You can find HRs' contacts either through friends who work in the company, or from social connections in LinkedIn.

If you are a student, check out your *university's career website*. It is very likely that there are internal job postings from big companies there. Submitting your resume there sometimes results in your resume being added to a separate pool which has high priority than the general submission from company's website. In addition, you should pay attention to the *career fair* in your university. A career fair is usually an express lane that helps you to land a job quickly, with fewer rounds of interviews and faster response.

For the companies that you do not have referrals for, *apply on the company's website*. Note that you should get prepared and act early, if you are newly graduating from school. Because many companies have an annual quota for new graduate hires. If you act late, you will not have chance to be considered once the positions are all filled.

One last thing we want to mention, before ending this chapter, is that *job seeking is a two-way selection process*. While employers are evaluating your qualification for the position, you should also select the right employer who can maximize your career growth. In order to do that, you should always proactively ask for more information about the job for which you are about to apply/interview. Ask your friends for the daily life and job responsibilities in the company. If HR contacts you, ask for contact of the hiring manager (HM), and talk with HM for more information about the position and the company. It will not only help you to better prepare for the interview but also let you know about whether the position is the right one for you, therefore you can stop early if it is not, without wasting the company's and your time to conduct the interview.

I will quote from one of my favorite books *The Alchemist*, by *Paulo Coelho*, to end this chapter:

> When you want something, all the universe conspires
> in helping you to achieve it.

Chapter 5

Polish Your Soft Skills

The interview process provides an opportunity for the candidate and the interviewer to communicate. The interviewer asks technical questions to see if there is a match between the candidate's technical background and the job requirements. All too often, the candidate being interviewed is focused solely on this technical portion of the interview, much to the neglect of the non-technical portion, which is tremendously relevant. Such a mistake is costly. During the interview process, the interviewer is constantly assessing your quality as a potential co-worker, taking cues to see if you would be a pleasant person to work with on a day-to-day basis, and trying to discern your personality type and how likable you are. That's when the subtle part of an interview comes into play. We often hear complaints like "I answered all the technical questions correctly, how did I not pass the interview?" You must take care not to neglect the human element of the interview process. Remember, you come to the interview room as a person, not a program. To put it this way: A customer cares most about whether or not the exact product he ordered is delivered to him. But how that product is delivered is also of importance. How many customers would choose a carrier pigeon over a UPS truck as their preferred shipping method?

So it is in the interview room. The interviewer wants to hear the right answer. But what good is it if you have the perfect answer, but cannot deliver it in the way they prefer? It's undeniable that a strong technical background can put you on a short list, but there are many candidates as qualified as you. Your soft skills will become the last straw in the hiring decision. Such things can make or break your opportunity. The authors hear hiring managers in the interview debrief panel saying: "Bill is a bit weaker than Raj in technical training. However, Bill is eager to learn, and it seems that he has greater potential to become an all-around data scientist. Conversely, Raj seems to have low energy. So I recommend hiring Bill instead of Raj." It is vitally important to be careful what signals you send through your tones and body gestures, and what personality you project in the interview process. This chapter discusses what the interviewers expect from candidate by asking non technical questions and how a candidate should present himself/herself in order to ace the interview and secure the dream job.

5.1 Expectations from behavior questions

Unlike technical questions, soft skill questions (or behavior questions) have no definitively correct answers. Some behavior questions are posed in the guise of a casual chat such as, "how do you persuade your boss to agree with your idea on a new project". But many other behavior questions are not directly asked. Instead, they are embedded in the interview process itself, and buried under other questions. Such hidden behavior questions are subliminal judgments of you from the interviewer. For instance, the interviewer has such questions constantly in his mind: Are you smart, are you easy-going, are you going to be a good team player or a potential leader in certain areas? Overall, the interviewer assesses the candidate in the following aspects.

5.1.1 Enthusiasm toward the products of the future employer

This is nearly the most important factor an interviewer or even an HR screen want to assess in their candidates. And you can easily spot such questions when they come up. For example, have you heard about us? Have you used our product X? Or even, why do you want to work for us? It would be a glaring red flag to the employer if you don't even know of or use any of the products of the company. In addition, the interviewer looks for unspoken signs of your interests and passions in the project, product, or the company throughout the interview process. A slight sign of disinterest from you would become a big red flag for interviewer. Only when you work on something you are passionate about, you will make a happy employee and a happy team member. The authors do see a lot of candidates going to interviews without prior exposures to the products of the company. Therefore, do some homework on the company before you interview. Express your genuine interests through the interview process. However, express your interest in a genuine manner and don't act like you are too eager or fervent to get the job. The authors also heard cases that the interview panel is turned off by overzealous candidates.

5.1.2   Culture fit

Each company has its own distinctive culture. And being able to accept and fit the culture of this company is a strong indicator that the candidate can survive and grow in the company a few years down the road. Some Internet companies, especially startups, are generally fast-paced and encourage tremendous ownership in the product and its features. For example, "Done is better than perfect" and "Move fast and break things" are mottos at Facebook. Someone who is an initiator, challenger, hacker, and risk-taker may be a good fit for these types of companies. On the other hand, established companies, especially business oriented companies may require skills of or-

ganization, communication, and collaboration. Someone who values work-life balance, financial stability, and well-defined job duties may be better suited to those companies. The interviewer may ask what you value in a work environment to determine if your priorities align with the company culture. Working for a company that has different values and priorities from yours only discourages innovation, reduces productivity, and dampens morale. Culture-fit questions are asked more and more in the data science job interviews. It shows interviewers are taking culture fit seriously in the interview process.

5.1.3 Presentation skills

It is never enough to emphasize the importance of communication and presentation skills as a data analyst/scientist. The data scientist usually works in an interdisciplinary team. The skills of effective verbal and written communication are essential to your day-to-day duty as a data scientist. Are you able to communicate your ideas to the executives or business people who may not have technical background? Are you able to convince the audience that the new findings from the dataset produced actionable insight? Are you able to write white papers and documentations for data science projects? The interviewer may look for evidence in your past experience for proven communication skills. Do you have any conference speaking experience? Have you published any papers in your technical domain? Interviewers can also assess presentation skills by asking about your past project or experience.

5.1.4   People skills

In companies with a sizable data science team, data analysts or scientists often work with each other on projects. Interviewers keep a keen eye on your ability to work in a team and what energy you would bring to the team if you are hired. If disagreements indeed arise, how would you react? If other team members need help, are you willing to lend a hand? Are you going to be a pleasant person to work with? The interviewers look for signs from a candidate possessing qualities such as collaboratively and amicability. In other companies, data analysts/scientists are expected to assume an all-around data officer role. As part of the day-to-day job, data scientists interact with different stakeholders— project managers, software engineers, and executives. Pulling people across varying job functions to execute an undertaking as complicated as a data science project and seeing to its successful delivery requires tremendous amount of listening, negotiation, organization, leadership, and patience. In interviewing with such companies, people skills are even more emphasized. Be prepared to present yourself with a level of maturity, sophistication, and shrewdness.

5.1.5 Attitude

Attitude is everything. A genuine, confident, and humble employee is an invaluable asset to a team. Interviewers are always looking for a candidate with honesty and integrity that the team can trust. They look for people who are determined but not overly stubborn, open minded but not lacking conviction, adaptive to new situations but also well organized. The interviewers like to see those qualities that will positively impact the team chemistry. Bringing in someone arrogant, albeit with strong technical background, will poison the well, and the interviewer knows it better than anybody else. So even if you feel you are overqualified for the position or the questions the interviewer asked are obvious, respond with respect and dignity. When asked difficult interview questions, keep calm and show your patience and persistence. Don't give up easily.

5.1.6 What kind of person you are

At the end of the day, by asking a set of questions, the interviewer is trying to get an idea what kind of person you are. Are you a listener or a speaker in a conversation? Are you passive or aggressive during discussions? Are you a follower or a leader in a group? In the interaction with the candidate, the interviewer makes his/her judgment if the chemistry is right—the chemistry between you and the interviewer, your skill set and the job requirements, your attitude and the team dynamics, your work style and the company culture. Different companies have different hiring philosophies. For example, Amazon adopts the idea of "hire someone better than you", while Facebook's Mark Zuckerberg has a different rule for hiring: "I will only hire someone to work directly for me if I would work for that person." And yet some companies only hire candidates if they can envision their employees enjoying them over a round of beer or a good lunch.

Interviewers are different, but they all assess what energy you would bring to the team and look for signs of the right chemistry.

5.2 Preparing non-technical questions

Unlike technical questions that might have a best solution, behavior questions are subjective and are often devoid of a standardized answer. However, there are tips one can follow to better prepare for the interview process.

5.2.1 Research the product, the team, and the company

It is essential to know the positions you applied for, the products the team is working on, and the business and culture of the company. When you first meet your interviewer, it is best to establish a conversation about their product or specialized area. If you demonstrate prior knowledge of their product, it creates an instant connection with the interviewer and shows your interest in the product. The authors heard a case in which a social network company rejected a candidate in a phone screening because the candidate did not have an account with the social network. In addition, researching the company culture before your interview also helps you decide if you will like working there if hired. Getting such information is easier than it sounds. Usually there are many websites like glassdoor.com with employees contributing their opinions and experience with the company. Once you secure the interview opportunity, it is a common practice to request that HR arrange a conversation with the hiring manager of the team you are hoping to join.

5.2.2 Summarize your contributions, impacts and learning from your past experience

Interviewers often look to start a conversation by asking questions about the candidate's past experience. When you explain the past project, the interviewer is given an opportunity to know your background; assess your technical depth, strengths, and contributions; and determine your ability to communicate ideas. Brush up on past projects you worked on and be prepared to answer any details and follow-up questions related to the projects.

It is often the interviewer's strategy to press on the details of the techniques used in past project in order to assess the candidate's technical depth and integrity. If you just say, "It is been a long time since I last worked on it so I don't remember," it does not leave the impression of a strong candidate. In addition, think about the challenges you solved and the lessons learned. The interviewer wants to know if you are a person who has learned from the past. Another important thing the interviewer wants to know from your past experience is the impact you have made on your past employers. This information will enable them to infer what values you can bring to the table on the new team. Therefore, present your past experience in a way that is not merely an explanation of a product or its technical details, but also the (potential) impact it makes. For example, what business metrics you have improved? What value do you bring to the customers? What the value you bring to your team?

5.2.3 Align your career goal with the new job

The interviewer may ask why you applied for the position. Be clear about your career goals and what you want to do with your skill set. Try to establish a relationship between your career goals and the job you are interviewing for. If you can align your interest, passion, and qualifications together with the job position, it will sound very convincing to the interviewer that you are qualified for the job. It also shows you know where you want to go career-wise and conveys your professional ambition, which is a big plus. Try to avoid ambivalence and ambiguity when talking about your goals. It exposes the lack of preparedness and motivation. However, be honest about your lack of experience in certain areas when asked, and show your interest in constant learning.

5.2.4   Answer with STAR (situation, task , action , response) method

STAR method is a popular interview technique that you can use in data science interviews. When asked questions like the biggest challenges you faced when doing a project, you can respond by taking advantage of the STAR method. Basically, STAR represents situation (S), task (T), action (A), and response (R). Talk about the challenging projects you faced before and the critical tasks you were responsible for solving. Talk about the ideas you had and actions you took to try to solve the problem and the difficulties encountered when doing so. Finally talk about the results you produced in the end, the contribution and impact you made and the learning experience you had. Using the STAR method in an appropriate manner conveys the image of a motivated executor and a problem solver. It provides a template for your thought process when answering similar behavior questions and it has been proven to be very effective.

5.2.5   Ask questions about your future job

More often than not, at the end of an interview, the interviewer asks if the candidate has any questions. You can take this opportunity to ask further questions regarding the product and project, or raise any other questions you have. If you have done your homework well in getting to know the company, the team and the product, it is always easy to think of excellent questions for the interviewer. By asking good questions at the end, it demonstrates your interests and knowledge, and it convinces the interviewer you are an active thinker. It is recommended to finish strong by asking a couple of questions if being offered the chance. Some sample questions to ask regarding the further details of the projects and products. For example, how many teammates are there in the team? How many headcounts the team has had this year? What technology or platform is the team is currently using? What past hackathon projects the interviewer was working on? An even better set of questions or comments might be your suggestions for improving the products (with added features) if you were to be hired for the job.

5.3 Selected sample behavior questions

Behavior questions take diverse forms and they vary greatly across companies and different job positions. Yet, they will always centered on your past experience, your future goals, and the job functions. Below, you will find a list of some of frequently asked behavioral questions in data science interviews. Think how you would answer these questions. Keep in mind the tips we have provided in this chapter. Think twice about your past experience and your career goals. Finally, try to answer them with STAR method.

- What's the most difficult project you have ever been involved with? What challenges did you have? How did you solve it? Did you seek help?

- Why do you want to work for this company? Why did you leave your last job?

- What kind of people do you prefer to work with? Do you like to work in a group setting?

- If you can't deliver the promised task in time, how will you communicate this to your boss?

- If you were passionate about an idea for a project, how would you convince your boss to agree with you?

- What's your biggest weakness?

- Why have you changed your jobs so often?

5.4   Taboos in handling non-technical questions

We discussed about the dos in the interview process. There is no single, silver bullet to a successful interview, but there are multiple ways to spoil an interview. Below, we list a few taboos in handling non-technical questions in the interview. You will want to avoid these at all costs. They either send the wrong signal or bring negativity to the process.

- Talk negative about your last employer. Speaking badly of your last employer in the interview process is a big red flag. Be honest about the reasons you are leaving your previous employer without trying to take anyone down.

- Lack of interests/passion for the job/position or being overzealous. This is one of the top few reasons why people are turned down by an interviewer.

- Inappropriate attire, language, gestures. It is an interview for a job. Be professional and show your best self.

- Asking your interviewer about your future salary or their personal information. You can ask about the compensation information when you get the chance to talk the HR, not to the interviewer. Mostly likely the interviewers don't know that either. If you want to make a connection with the interviewer, there are better conversation topics such as projects, programming languages, and technology tools etc.

- Lying about your experience. Integrity is everything. If you are found out to be lying about your experience, you lose all trust. Once lost, trust is exceedingly difficult to regain. Don't even be tempted.

- Leak confidential information or other information under NDA (Non-Disclosure Agreements) with your past employer. It is not legal or ethical to talk about the information that is still under NDA from your last employer. The interviewer wouldn't want to know that either. If you can't keep promise, it is a big red flag.

In summary, the data science interview is a holistic and organic process. While being well prepared for the technical questions is necessary, the non-technical portion of the interview is also critical. It is your opportunity to shine as the person you are. Just take it as an opportunity to communicate with the interviewer and present your best self. The interview process is a two-way street. At the end of day, you want to know more about the product, the features, and business of your future employer. You also want to know if the job aligns with your interests. Furthermore, you can exercise your judgment to see if the job can provide you the career opportunities you want. You can also ponder if the company's culture and values are a good fit for you.

Chapter 6

Technical Interview Questions

This book aims to help you prepare for data science job interviews and land your dream job. The authors of the book have been on both sides of the table – as interviewers and as interviewees – and have unique insights in the data science interview process. We present questions that cover basic statistics and probability concepts, data manipulation and coding skills, experiment design, product sense, and problem solving.

An interview is not a pop quiz. You should take the time to practice on real interview problems and learn their patterns. During the interview loop, the recruiter is on your side and is trying to maximize your chance of getting an offer so that he or she will get the bonus. You should ask your recruiter what types of interviews you will have. Even recruiters may be reluctant to share that – they usually will send you some good general guides for what would happen during the interviews.

Here are some types of questions you might encounter during the interviews:

Probability and Statistics

This is the core of what you can offer as a data scientist. You should be familiar with basic probability theory and statistical inference concepts, such as combinatory event probability, conditional probability, expected value, confidence intervals, parameter estimation, p-value, t-test, A/B test and other hypothesis testing. You should have a decent intuitive understanding of statistics. A common sample question of this type is how to set up an A/B test to see whether a new product feature is better than the existing one or not, including random sampling, covariate variables, and aggregation moments (e.g. mean), and statistical significance. You should also be able to describe a probability/statistics topic from your resume to a non-specialist. As a data scientist or data analyst, it's crucial to have the communication and presentation skills to convey your ideas and thoughts to someone who is not a domain expert.

Dataset Manipulation

In this type of interview questions, you will be given some database tables, and be asked to write a script (mostly SQL) to pull out related information. Some common questions include joining tables, making use of sub-queries, and aggregating data statistics (moments or ranks) using GROUP BY. You need to understand the difference between INNER JOIN and JOIN, the difference between WHERE and HAVING. Please pay attention to rows that might have NULL column, and make sure you understand the approximate cost of each SQL execution step.

Experiment Design

Almost every company asks about A/B testing in experiment design interview questions. This is because A/B testing plays a vital role in modern Internet companies when it comes to testing new website features and tracking their performance and metrics. However, candidates who are just fresh out of school usually have not encountered this technology before. Therefore we select experiment design questions that range from basic statistical concepts to more advanced applications in this chapter. We hope candidates can get a flavor on how experiment design is used and where the companies are interested to test their future candidates.

Product, Metrics and Analytics

Questions in this section are another type that are not covered by textbooks and standard curriculum. Yet product metrics and analysis are used in most data science jobs. The questions in this chapter are designed to get candidates familiar with the scenarios where interviewers ask about products. Because those questions are typically open ended, the answers we provide aim to address a few perspectives of how to answer those questions well and impress the interviewers. We also list several common metrics that many Internet companies usually evaluate their products on. Candidates are highly encouraged to explore further based on those metrics.

Coding

Some social network companies such as Facebook, Twitter, and LinkedIn require data science job candidates to have excellent coding skills. You should get comfortable with fundamental algorithms and algorithm time/space complexity. Usually you have the freedom to code in any "real" programming language (Matlab doesn't count, unfortunately). This type of interview questions is similar to software engineer interview questions, while the expectations might be less stringent. There are lots of websites (e.g.: `leetcode.com`, `hackerrank.com`) and books (*Cracking the Coding Interview*) that help you to prepare. Don't forget to practice coding without using the computer since most coding interviews during onsite will require you to write code on the whiteboard. Get comfortable with basic programming concepts like control flow, loop iteration and recursion will definitely help. Know how to reason about the algorithms' time complexity is better. Python's succinct syntax makes it ideal for coding interviews. We present solutions to the selected coding questions in the book using Python.

During the interview, sometimes the question is not well defined. Make sure you understand exactly what the problem is about. Ask the interviewer questions for clarity if you have any doubts. Communicate with your interviewer about the prerequisite, conditions, input, and output before you start writing any code. Don't get nervous if you can't think of a good way to solve the problem. It often helps to start with a naive/brute-force method to solve the problem. Before finishing your code, think about corner cases (e.g. empty inputs) by running through some examples.

Machine Learning

Some data science interviews, especially those for data scientist positions, require machine learning expertise. To prepare machine learning questions, you should be able to explain basic machine learning concepts on an intuitive level, focusing especially on supervised learning. For example, explain the trade-off between bias and variance; what is overfitting and how to prevent it; why it's necessary to split data into training and test sets; and what is the math behind linear regression, logistic regression and their variants.

Sometimes interviewers will ask you to apply machine learning techniques to solve a real life problem that is relevant to the company's business and explain how you would choose a proper machine learning algorithm. At the end of the day, what the companies expect to see is your ability to use algorithms to discover insights from data, and to build a service to make decisions or predictions based on data. This type of interview questions evaluates not only candidates' understanding of machine learning concepts, but also their communication skills. You need to discuss with the interviewer about the setup of the problem, i.e., what are the inputs, what are the labels you're trying to predict, what is the scale of training data, and what are the most important features.

In the following sections, we will briefly introduce and then present interview questions on topics including: probability theory, statistical inference, dataset manipulation, product, metrics and analytics, experiment design, coding, machine learning, and brain teasers. All the questions are either real interview questions or adapted from real interview questions that were asked at leading technology companies. Detailed solutions and hints for each question are provided in Chapter 7. We hope readers can grasp the key points behind each of them, hence be able to apply the approaches to other similar questions in real interviews. Note that, some questions, like product metric and experiment design questions, may have more than one valid solutions. We provide hints as well as sample solutions. Meanwhile, readers are highly encouraged to think out of the box and explore alternative solutions.

6.1   Probability Theory

Introduction

Problems in this section assess your ability to apply basis probability theory to analyze real world problems. The central concepts in probability theory are sample space, events, random variables, conditional probability, Bayes' theorem, and others. We know that probability is a mathematical tool to analyze random phenomena, whose outcomes are subject to variations due to chance or randomness. The set of all possible outcomes or results of a random phenomenon is called the sample space. A subset of the sample space to which a probability is assigned is called an event. Combinatorial methods are generally used to compute probabilities of discrete events.

A random variable is a function defined on a sample space, which maps events to numerical values (probabilities). A conditional probability $\Pr(A|B)$ measures the probability of an event A assuming that the other event B has occurred. Let A and B denote two events, $\Pr(A)$ and $\Pr(B)$ are the probabilities of A and B, respectively. Bayes' theorem states that:

$$\Pr(A|B) = \frac{\Pr(B|A)\Pr(A)}{\Pr(B)}$$

In the Bayesian interpretation of probability theory, the probability of an event measures the degree of belief over that event. However, such degree of belief is subject to change given some evidence has occurred. Bayes' theorem shows how the degree of belief in event A changed before (the prior $\Pr(A)$) and after (the posterior $\Pr(A|B)$) accounting for evidence B.

Most questions in this chapter are about computing conditional probabilities and applying Bayes' rule. Generally speaking, questions in this category are more like simple puzzles that don't require too much knowledge in probability theory. Venn diagram or tree graphs are useful to visualize the probabilities of multiple events.

6.1.1 Coin Flipping

If you keep throwing a fair coin, how many times on average do you need to flip to get two consecutive observations of the same side (both heads or both tails)?

6.1.2 Biased Coin

Given 10 coins with 1 biased coin and 9 fair coins. The biased coin has probability $p > 0.5$ to be head. Now randomly pick one coin and throw it three times. The observation sequence is head, head, and tail. What's the probability that the selected coin is the biased one?

6.1.3   Fair Result from a Biased Coin

Suppose you are given a biased coin, which has probability $p > 0.5$ to be head. How can you use this biased coin to get a fair coin toss. More specifically, how do you use this biased coin to generate a sequence of heads and tails in which the probability of getting a head is the same as the probability of getting a tail.

6.1.4   Dice Payout

You are allowed to roll a dice at most three times. You will receive x dollars reward where x is the highest roll you get. You can choose to stop rolling at any time. For example, you get a six on you first roll then you can stop. What is the expected payout?

6.1.5   Finding Tesla

During the lunchtime suppose you are sitting by the street, you find that there is 64% chance observing at least one Tesla in one hour. What is the probability that you observe at least one Tesla in half an hour?

6.1.6   Mark Balls

There are 100 balls with #1 - #100 mark on each of them.

Each ball has its number marked on it. Now let's define a process P as: randomly choose a ball, if the ball already has a star on it, put it back, otherwise mark the ball with a star and then put it back.

1. After repeating the process P for 100 times, find the ball that is marked with number #1. What is the probability that the ball doesn't have a star on it?

2. What is the number of times that you need to repeat this process P, if you want to get all the balls marked with star.

6.1.7 Playoff Games

Say there are two teams, A and B. The probability A wins is p. The series ends after 4 games if one team wins all four games. What is the probability of 7-game series? What p maximizes the probability of 7-game series?

6.1.8   Rolling A Four

What is the probability of rolling a 4 with 2 dice? What's the probability of rolling at least one 4 out of 2 dice.

6.1.9   Broken Computers

Your department has 20 computers and 4 of them are broken. If we randomly sample 12 computers from those 20 (without replacement), what is the probability of getting at least 3 broken computers?

6.1.10   Ant Collisions

Three ants are sitting at the three corners of an equilateral triangle. Each ant randomly picks a direction and starts to move along the edge of the triangle. What is the probability that none of the ants collide? Follow-up: k ants are sitting at the k corners of an equilateral polygon. Each ant randomly picks a direction and starts to move along the edge of the polygon. What's the probability that none of the ants collide?

6.1.11   American Family

Let X be the number of children in an ordinary American family. Let $\Pr(X = i) = p_i$, for $i = 1, 2, 3, 4$, and $\Pr(X > 4) = 0$, what is the probability that there are at least two girls in a family?

6.2 Statistical Inference

Introduction

Statistical Inference assumes the observed data is from a larger population and aims to derive the properties of the distribution of the larger population. It is different from descriptive statistics that solely studies the properties of observed data.

Statistical Inference has two steps. The first step is to choose or formulate the conclusion of the inference. Usually the conclusion takes the form of the following:

- point estimation, e.g. the probability someone has certain diseases.

- confidence interval estimation, e.g. the confidence interval of your point estimate.

- rejection of hypothesis, e.g. whether two groups of user behaviors are the same.

The second step is choosing an assumption or a model to derive the above conclusions. Here are some common models, assumptions and derivation models:

- Bayesian rules for estimating posterior and likelihood or conditional probability

- Non-parametric models or semi-parametric models which assumes underlying data has a certain distribution or do not assume any distribution. For example, using linear regression model to approximate posterior probability assumes the normality of error distribution; random forest is a powerful non-parametric model to estimate the posterior probability or point estimate directly.

- Fully parametric models which assumes the full distributions of the data generation process with unknown parameters. For example, modeling customer purchases as Poisson distribution with unknown lambda. Common parametric distributions and the meanings of the parameters can be found here[1]. It's also important to know the relationships between common distributions [2]. It's especially useful when someone applied *conjugate priors* to update the posterior distribution based on the prior distribution and the likelihood of observed evidence using Bayer' rule.

Statistical inference has numerous applications in the day-to-day job in data science. Case I: we want to verify our hypothesis using a data set e.g. whether the sets of collected measurement have statistically significant difference. Case II: we want to derive estimates from data set to make decisions, e.g., given the customer has these set of events on the website, what advertisement should be served to him or her? When it comes to interview questions about statistical inference, first, interviewers are often

---

[1]http://aleph0.clarku.edu/~djoyce/ma218/distributions.pdf
[2]http://en.wikipedia.org/wiki/Relationships_among_probability_distributions

interested in whether the candidate is able to correctly formulate the answer of the question into the right statistical inference; e.g., whether it is a hypothesis testing or it is in fact estimating a conditional probability, a joint probability and so on. Second, they want to assess the candidate can use certain model and assumptions to be able to derive the answer. In this step, they will almost always question the choice of model and distribution assumption. Candidates should give some thoughts why making certain choices and be able to communicate the pros and cons.

Questions in this chapter are some typical types of questions using different statistical inference conclusions and parametric and no parametric models.

6.2.1 Disease Diagnosis

You're testing for a rare disease, with 1% of the population is infected. You have a highly sensitive and specific test: 99% of sick patients test positive, and 99% of healthy patients test negative. Given that a patient tests positive, what is the probability that the patient is actually sick?

6.2.2 Maximize Click Through Rate

Assume you are about to start an email campaign about your company's latest product. You can choose to send out emails to potential customers at anytime, for instance, 6am, 2pm, and 11pm. When to send emails to users so that you can get maximum click through rate (CTR)?

6.2.3   Is This Coin Unfair?

Given a coin you don't know it's fair or unfair. Throw it 6 times and get 1 tail and 5 head. Determine whether it's fair or not. What's your confidence value?

6.2.4   Yes, It Is Raining

You're about to get on a plane to Seattle. You want to know if you should bring an umbrella. You call 3 random friends of yours who live there and ask each independently if it's raining. Each of your friends has a 2/3 chance of telling you the truth and a 1/3 chance of messing with you by lying. All 3 friends tell you that "Yes" it is raining. What is the probability that it's actually raining in Seattle?

6.3 Dataset Manipulation

Introduction

Before performing any data analysis, the first step is always to get the right data. Structured Query Language, known for SQL, is the most popular language for data extraction and aggregation. There are lots of different SQL languages, such as Oracle SQL, PostgreSQL, T-SQL, MySQL, and others. They are extensions of the standard SQL, with slight differences in syntax and functionalities. Normally the interviewer will not specify a particular SQL language during the interview. But the interviewees need to equip themselves with at least one SQL language, its syntax and unique functionalities.

During the interviews, the interviewer is likely to test in following areas of SQL:

- Table schema design for transactional database; data manipulation; query optimization

- Key concepts in SQL including different types of *JOIN*; Aggregate functions working with *GROUP BY*; using *RANK* function with *OVER* clause, and others.

In this chapter, we give sample interview questions on SQL and data manipulation. Solutions to each of them, which are written mainly in MySQL or PostgreSQL, can be found in Chapter 7.

6.3.1   Consecutive Number

Assume a MySQL table "logs" with columns timestamp and jobID. The table log contains information about the history of job failures. Find all the jobIDs that appear at least twice consecutively. Please answer in a single query and assume read-only access to the database (i.e. do not use CREATE TABLE).

Table Names: logs	
Column Name	Data type
timestamp	Integer
jobID	Integer

For example, given the table:

timestamp	jobID
1	1
2	2
3	1
4	1
5	3
6	2
7	1
8	4

the only jobID that appears twice consecutively is 1. Once you answer this question, the interviewer might extend the question to arbitrary k: find all jobIDs that appear at least k times consecutively.

6.3.2 Music Actions

Assume we have a PostgreSQL database. Given two tables music_action and summary_table.

- Summarize that, for each client, how many pieces of music (including duplicate ones) do they listen to so far?

- Write a function to update the summary_table using the music_action table with the latest snapshotDay.

Please answer in a single query and assume read only access to the database (i.e. do not use CREATE TABLE).

The music_action is a table recording daily music listened by clients.

Table Names: music_action	
Column Name	Data type
actionID	Integer
clientID	Integer
musicID	Integer
snapshotDay	Timestamp

and the summary_table is:

Table Names: summary_table	
Column Name	Data type
clientID	Integer
numPlay	Integer
musicID	Integer
endDate	Timestamp

The summary_table is an accumulative table, which means each row is the number of times each clientID listened to musicID up to endDate.

6.3.3 No Sales

Create three tables a) *accounts*, which contains accountid b) *dates*, which contains dateid c) *facts*, which contains three columns date, accountid and revenue. The facts table records the expense of an account every day if there is expense. If there is no expense then there won't be a record in the facts table. Given this scenario write a SQL query that generates a list of all Accounts on every day in the last 30 days that had no expense.

6.3.4 Second Highest Sale

Assume we have a PostgreSQL database, and a table Sales, which is a table with product and sales information. Write a SQL query to find out the second highest sale from the Sales table. Please answer in a single query and assume read-only access to the database (i.e. do not use CREATE TABLE).

Table Names: Sales	
Column Name	Data type
productID	Integer
sale	Numeric

If there is no second highest salary, then the query should return NULL. Once this problem is solved, interviewer will most likely increase the difficulty level by either moving to get the Kth sale or taking away some database specific built-in features like TOP, LIMIT, or ROW_NUMBER.

6.3.5 TF–IDF

Given a corpus table with columns pageid, text, for example, all Wikipedia documents keyed by pageid, write HIVE/MYSQL queries to calculate the tfidf of each word.

6.3.6 Top K Sales

Assume a PostgreSQL database. Given schema Sales, which is a table with product and sales information. Write executable SQL queries to find out top 3 products for each category in terms of sales on a daily basis. Please answer in a single query and assume read-only access to the database (i.e. do not use CREATE TABLE).

Table Names: Sales	
Column Name	Data type
ProductID	Integer
ProductName	CHAR(50)
Sales	Numeric
SalesDate	Date
Category	CHAR(20)

6.4   Product, Metrics and Analytics

Introduction

Product and Metrics related interview questions might not be familiar to candidates who recently step into data science job market. These questions are frequently asked in data science job interviews, especially in data scientist and data analyst interviews. Interviewers use product questions to test candidates' thought process – whether they can think logically and systematically, whether they are capable of dealing with ambiguity. In most cases, product questions are closely related to real life products, and it could be one of the past/current problems the interviewer had/has worked on. Generally, the interviewer starts with a simple case scenario, and will give more conditions based on candidate's response along the process. For this type of questions, interviewer and job candidate work together to explore the open-end questions.

When the interviewer explains the scenario to you, often times it does not contain all the related information. At first, interviewer will give a brief description of the setup for the question. However, the setup might not be 100% clear. For instance, the question might be as vague as "There is a big drop in the advertisement click through rate", "how do you diagnose this problem". This one sentence setup is too broad to tackle directly; you might have several question marks in your head. In this circumstance, it is a good idea to speak up. Thus, it is vital for candidates to ask anything that is not clear. You could start with some questions such as "how big is the drop", "could I look into the past time series rate to check whether this is abnormal or not", "is there a national holiday when the drop occurs". Asking questions helps you refine and identify the problem.

When you raise question about the problem, the interviewer

would answer most of them. Pay attention to these feedbacks, this will help you make valid assumptions. In many product related interviews, you are not given the real data set. Thus, there are potentially a lot of assumptions that need to be made in order for you to move forward. It is a good practice to keep your assumptions in mind, so that when you get follow-up questions, you can answer consistently.

The interviewer may integrate some conceptual questions into product questions. For instance, during the discussion, if the candidate mentions using t-test to detect whether there is an improvement after implementing a new method. The interviewer may follow up with questions like "what is t-test", "how do you implement t-test in this case". Thus, as an interviewee, you need to be prepared for the concepts you mention. However, if you are not sure about some concepts, do not pretend that you know it well, be honest and if needed, ask the interviewer for hints.

Different from probability or coding questions, product questions usually do not have standard answers. It is vital for the interviewees to explore different possibilities. In most cases, there is not absolute evaluation of right and wrong. Don't be afraid to say anything wrong. The interviewers may challenge your assumptions and conclusions, or bring cases you haven't yet thought about. Being challenged is common and natural. It is not a bad thing. Don't panic. Calm down, remember your assumptions, use hints, and integrate corner cases.

Facebook Full Year 2014 Business Highlights

Revenue for the full year 2014 was $12.47 billion, an increase of 58% year-over-year. Income from operations for the full year 2014 was $4.99 billion. Net income for the full year 2014 was $2.94 billion. Free cash flow for the full year 2014 was $3.63 billion. Daily active users (DAUs) were 890 million on average for December 2014, an increase of 18Mobile DAUs were 745 million on average for December 2014, an increase of 34% year-over-year. Monthly active users (MAUs) were 1.39 billion as of December 31, 2014, an increase of 13% year-over-year. Mobile MAUs were 1.19 billion as of December 31, 2014, an increase of 26% year-over-year.[a]

[a]http://newsroom.fb.com/company-info

Product questions are always closely tight to metrics. What are metrics about? In high tech industry, what's the measurement of success? Have you heard people discussing about CTR, exit page, active users and were not sure what they are talking about? Being familiar with commonly used metrics requires hands-on working experiences. To help new graduates and people transferring from other areas quickly ramp up in this area, we will discuss some fundamental metrics and their applications in the following sections.

Let's first take a sneak at Facebook's Full Year 2014 Business Highlights from Fourth Quarter and Full Year 2014 Financial Summary. It will give us a sense about how metrics are tight to describing company performance:

In the Business Highlights, it uses the company's revenue, income, net income, free cash flow, daily active users, mobile daily active users, monthly users, and mobile monthly users as the measurement of success. The rest of the section explains when some of them mean, as well as some other key metrics.

Active User:
> The number of active users is an important metrics to measure the success of an online product or website. It answers the questions like, how many unique users log on to the website or use the product within a certain period. Depending on the length of the period, two most popular metrics are daily active users –unique users who log on to the website or engage with the product within the previous day, and monthly active users – unique users who log on to the website or engage with the product at least once within the previous month. Let's look at an example. If we go to Facebook's company information webpage [3], we will see the following statistics. Under the section of Statistics, it describes the user base for Facebook: it has 890 million daily active users on average for December 2014, and it has 1.39 billion monthly active users as of December 31, 2014. What does it mean? It means on average, on one day in December 2014, there were about 890 million Facebook users logged in their Facebook accounts at least once. Meanwhile, there were 1.39 million Facebook users logged in their Facebook accounts at least once during December.

---

[3]http://newsroom.fb.com/company-info/

Conversion Rate:

Conversion Rate is widely used in various situations, and it has different interpretations under them. For instance, in E-commerce, it measures the percentage of visitors who finally purchase the products or services.

Impression:

Impression is a metric measuring how many people actually see the page, advertisement, or product. For instance, let's say you have 600 friends on Facebook. When you post a picture on Facebook, you might wonder how many people actually see this picture. If there are 200 friends who actually viewed the picture, the impression of your picture is 200.

Click Through Rate:

In advertisement, having lots of impression is not good enough. Click Through Rate, a.k.a. CTR, is also a key metric. It is the percentage of people who click into an advertisement out of people who see it. The formula for calculating the CTR is:

$$CTR = \frac{Clicks}{Impressions} \times 100\%$$

As business owner, you not only care about how many people see your advertisement, you also very interested in whether they engage with this ads and click into it, get more information or convert to customers.

Bounce Rate:

When people land on a website, they will choose to either stay or explore the other pages within the website or leave without further actions. Bounce rate is the percentage of people who leave a website or a webpage after they visit it, without continuing on to visit other pages within the same site.

Revenue:

Revenue is the amount of income a company or business entity receives from its business opportunity. In the case of Amazon, it is the amount of income they make from Retail, Cloud Service, Device, etc. Be aware that revenue is not the final amount of money falling into business entity's pocket. It is the number before various costs are deducted from.

Profit:

Profit is the surplus remaining after total costs have been deducted from revenue. It is financial gain from transactions or from a period of investment or business activity.

Above are explanations about selected metrics. In the following sections, we will present some sample product and metrics questions to help you get familiar with this type of questions, be prepared.

6.4.1 New Messenger App

An Internet company recently enforced users to use a standalone Messenger App and deprecated the chat functionality on the company's mobile App. To track the performance of this move, what metrics will you use?

6.4.2 Incorrectly Implemented Search Algorithm

To test a new search relevance algorithm, we performed an A/B testing. The control group would see search results returned by original algorithm, while the treatment group would see search results returned by new algorithm. During the process of A/B testing, engineers realized that the new algorithm was not fully validated and it was not implemented correctly, which resulted in lower relevance in search results than the original one does. Due to this, the test was terminated. However, when data scientist looked at this A/B testing result, surprisingly, on average people in treatment group performed more search queries than people in control group. Meanwhile, the advertising revenue was higher in treatment group than in control group.

Question 1:How would you explain that the new algorithm results in people performing more searches than the original algorithm? (Follow-up questions can be seen in Chapter 7 together with the solutions to this question)

6.4.3   Reduce Gas Efficiency

Assume Country M depends heavily on foreign oil. One of the major consumption comes from cars.

There are two types of cars, A and B. The number of people in Country M who use A and B are the same. They drive similar distances each month. Good news comes that there are two new technologies, X and Y (of equal cost). If applying X, mpg (mile per gallon) of A would increase from 50 mpg to 75 mpg. If applying Y, mpg of B would increase from 10 mpg to 11 mpg. The goal is to decrease the gasoline consumption. At this moment, Country M could only afford one of the new technologies, either X or Y.

Question 1: As the consultant of the president, which technology would you recommend to use?

Question 2: After applying the technology of your choice, assuming there is more fund available for research on new technology, which car would you choose to conduct research for?

6.5 Experiment Design

Introduction

Experiment design in statistics is often referred in the context of controlled experiments. In controlled experiments, the goal is to study the effect of some processes, interventions or strategies on experimented objects, which can be people, animals and plants and physical objects etc. Hypothesis testing techniques such as t test or ANOVA test are usually applied in experiment design to formalize the procedure and analyze the results.

Experiment design has found many applications in social science and engineering, especially when testing on people subjects. In modern companies, experiment design usually takes the form on A/B testing, a controlled experiment where A and B refer to two variants of products or services, with one being control and the other being treatment. They are usually identical in every aspect except for one variation which might lead to different user responses. We can also have more than two variants at a time. The goal is to test whether applying the treatment will result in significant difference (increase or decrease) in a set of predefined metrics (in some circumstance we call them success metrics), compared to the control group. For example, one can use A/B testing to test whether a newer version of webpage design will result in higher CTR (click through rate) compared to the current design. With the null hypothesis being that the two designs are the same, being able to reject this null hypothesis using A/B testing means control and treatment are truly different in CTR.

A/B testing plays a critical role in company operation and development. It is by far the best quantitative tool to test company strategies and products and to quantify their real world impacts, before an official and full launch. Modern companies iterate their products fast by putting different versions of prototypes in front of real users to distinguish the true business opportunities from the risk of investing wrongly.

A/B testing is a canonical example of how data and computing drive the ultimate business decisions. Therefore, as job candidates in data science, you are not only expected to be familiar with the general ideas and concepts of experiment design and A/B testing, but also expected to know the nuts and bolts about them, including:

- The statistical theory behind hypothesis testing. Frequently asked questions are significance, confidence interval, p value, t test, the definition of t statistics, effect size, power, two types of errors, A/A testing and A/B testing.

- The criteria and issues of samples and the importance of randomization. The power of an A/B test usually relates to the number of samples, which can be primary concern of real world applications and of interviewers.

- Multiple comparisons or testing. It is not rare that besides control there are multiple treatments to be tested simultaneously. Interviewers will be interested in knowing how to set up such experiments, what the limitations of multiple testing are, and how to address them.

- Some common interesting metrics that are being measured when running A/B testing on specific features, products and processes.

The questions below and their variants are frequently asked among interviews for data scientist, business analyst and business intelligence engineers. These questions can help you to better prepare for the subject of experiment design.

6.5.1 The Power of A Statistical Test

What is the definition of power? What are some factors that affect the power of the test? How does the power of the test relate to p-value in a certain test?

6.5.2 Sixty Four Designs

A website is testing its new designs of a page. They came up with 63 designs. Together with current design there are 64 different designs. They want to test all of them and choose the best. How will you set up the experiments, and calculate and report the results?

6.5.3 The Lovely New Feature

We want to add a new feature to our product. How to determine whether people like it or not?

6.5.4 Your Samples Are Biased

How do you know if your sample is biased? What would you do if your sample is actually biased?

6.6   Coding

Introduction

Data related positions usually require basic coding skills. Here we cover technical questions that assess programming concepts such as if else control flow, loop iterations, and recursions. More advanced data structure and algorithm analysis are generally required for software developer positions and thus are beyond the scope of this book. We present solutions to coding questions in Python.

6.6.1   Binary Sequence Decoding

We use a sequence of 1 to encode a message. 11 represents a k, 1 represents a a. Suppose we receive a sequence of 1 with length N, how many different phrases can we decode?

6.6.2   Majority Element

Given an array with size n, a *majority element* is an element that appears more than $\lceil n/2 \rceil$ times. Write a function that returns the majority element if it exists, otherwise returns None/NULL.

6.6.3   Pow(x, n)

Implement pow(x, n) where x is a double and n is an integer.

6.6.4   Remove Element

Given an array and a target value, remove all instances that equal to target value and return the new length. This should be done in place. The order of elements can be changed. It doesn't matter what you leave beyond the new length.

For example, given an array $\{1, 2, 3, 2, 5\}$ and a target value 2. Your program should return 3 and modify the array such that the first 3 elements of the array are not 2.

6.6.5 Running Median

Given a stream of integers, return the median of numbers every time a new number is added. For example, integers coming in the following order: $[4, 6, 1, 3, 2, 0]$, then the function will return $[4, 4, 4, 3, 3, 2]$.

6.6.6 Stock Prices

Given an array storing the historical prices of a stock where the ith element of the array represents the stock price at the ith hour, design an algorithm to find when to buy and sell one share of the stock to achieve the maximum profit. You are allowed to complete one transaction at most.

Follow up, what's the maximum profit you get if at most k transactions are allowed. k can be $2, 3, \ldots$ up to the number of elements of the array.

6.6.7   Two Sum

Given an array of integers, and a target T. Find two numbers in the array such that the sum equals to T. The function twoSum takes inputs of an array of integers and a target value; return the indices of two numbers, where index1 must be less than index2. You may assume that each input would have exactly one solution. What if the input array is sorted?

6.6.8   CTR Estimation Using Map-Reduce

You are asked to compute the click through rate (CTR) for advertisement from a large number of page logs. Each page log contains information such as ad_id (Integer type), is_shown (boolean type), and is_click (boolean type). How to compute the CTR for each ad as well as the overall CRT, using the map-reduce framework.

6.7 Machine Learning

Introduction

Machine learning has applications in a broad range of domains including online ad click predictions, web page rankings, revenue forecasting, fraud detection, and sentiment analysis. Many companies incorporate machine learning in their products such as search engines, social networks and e-commerce. Machine learning models have the power in finding patterns, trends, and anomalies in data, therefore data science jobs apply machine learning extensively. Interviewers often ask machine learning questions in the following areas:

- The underlying mathematical fundamentals of machine learning models.

- The advantages and limitations of each machine learning method.

- The feature engineering process.

- The evaluation and validation of results of the machine learning models

- Problem solving using machine learning methods.

Popular machine learning methods such as decision tree, logistic regression, linear regression, support vector machine are among the most asked models and techniques. Understanding the details of these methods is critical to interview success. Depending on the area of expertise, interviewers may ask advanced topics such as pattern recognition, natural language processing and deep learning.

Machine learning can be roughly divided into supervised learning and unsupervised learning depending on weather the model requires pre-labeled data to be built. Supervised learning can be divided into classification and regression depending if the prediction target is continuous or categorical. Unsupervised learning does not require a training set, for example clustering tasks fall in this category. Especially in questions of problem solving, candidates are advised to formulate the problem into supervised or unsupervised learning first, before choosing the right model to solve it.

6.7.1   Decision Tree

Answer the following questions regarding to the decision tree model.

1. How does decision tree decide the splitting criteria? Can we use decision tree for regression? What are the splitting criteria for decision tree regression?

2. When a feature X in the data set is a continuous random variable with probability density function $p(x)$, which is a Gaussian distribution with mean μ and variance σ^2, please derive its entropy $H(X)$. Name one property of the entropy you derived above that doesn't hold for any discrete random variable.

3. What are the advantages of decision trees?

4. If one of the features has very high cardinality (the number of values), how will it affect the decision tree model building process?

5. What are the main differences between boosting trees and random forest?

6. Write a simple program to generate a decision tree given X, XValues and Y. X is a $N \times D$ matrix of training features

where each row is an example and each column is a feature. The values of each feature are comparable and have only limited number of distinct values. XValues is a $D \times V$ matrix for all distinct feature values. Each row represents all possible distinct values of a feature. Y is an $N \times 1$ vector of labels. Suppose there already exists a function to compute the information gain.

6.7.2 Linear Regression

What is the basic assumption of using a linear regression? How do you empirically access that your distribution is normal? What are the most common estimation techniques for linear regression?

6.7.3 Logistic Regression

What's the formula for a logistic regression? How to determine the coefficients given the data?

6.7.4 Multi-class Logistic Regression

Assume that we have K different labels and each data point x has d dimensional features. The posterior probability for label k is then:

$$\Pr[Y = k | X = x] = \frac{\exp(W_k^T x)}{1 + \sum_{i=1}^{K-1} \exp(W_i^T x)}$$

for $k = 1, \ldots, K - 1$.

1. How many parameters do we need to estimate? What are these parameters?

2. Given n training samples, please write down explicitly the log likelihood function.

3. Compute the gradient of L with respect to each w_k and simply it.

4. Add the L^2 regularization term $\frac{\lambda}{2} \sum_i ||w_l||^2$, compute the gradient of the new cost function f.

6.7.5 Naive Bayes

1. Given the training data (X, y), what assumptions do the Naive Bayes methods make?

2. Suppose X is a vector of n boolean features and y is a discrete variable with m possible values, let $\theta_{ij} = P(X_i|y = y_j)$. What's the number of independent θ_{ij} parameters. Now suppose X is a vector of n continuous features and $P(X_i = x_i|y = y_j) \sim N(x_i|\mu_{ij}, \sigma_{ij})$. How many distinct μ_{ij}, σ_{ij} are there?

3. Write maximum likelihood estimator (MLE) estimator for θ_{ij}.

6.7.6 Neural Network

Suppose there is a neural network with two input units X_1 and X_2, two hidden units h_1 and h_2, and an output unit o_1. The weights between X_1 and the two hidden units are w_1 and w_3, the weights between X_2 and the hidden units are w_4 and w_2. The weights between the output unit and hidden units are w_5 and w_6. There is no bias term in those units.

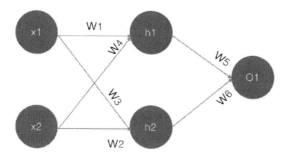

1. Suppose this network uses only linear activation functions. That is, the output of a unit is a linear combination of its inputs, weighted by the weights. For example, $h_1 = w_1 X_1 + w_4 X_2$. Redesign the network without any hidden units to compute the same function.

2. Is it possible to combine a multi-layered (deep) neural network with linear activation function into a single layer one without any hidden layer?

3. The activation of the neuron can be arbitrary. Suppose in our network, the activation function for the hidden units is the sigmoid function, which is $\frac{1}{1+\exp(-\sum_i w_i x_i)}$. The output of the output neuron, however, returns 1 only if the sum of the inputs from hidden units is greater than 0. Find the weights of this network so that it can output X_1 XOR X_2 where X_1 and X_2 are binary.

6.7.7 Overfitting

What are some of the issues you encounter when training machine learning models? What's overfitting? Have you ever overfitted your data? What causes overfitting? How to overcome overfitting?

6.7.8 Regression Evaluation

How do you evaluate regression? In an online item click tracking system. We would like to predict the item click through rate (CTR). Some actual and predicted is shown in the table below:

ID	Actual CTR	Predicted CTR
1	005	0.06
2	0.69	0.78
3	0.22	0.19
4	0.58	0.57
...	...	...

How would you calculate the CTR prediction performance?

6.7.9 Support Vector Machine

1. What is a support vector machine?

2. What are the support vectors?

3. What differentiates it from other linear classifiers, such as the Linear Perceptron, Linear Discriminant Analysis, or Logistic Regression?

4. Describe three kernel functions and when to use which of them.

6.8 Brain Teasers

Introduction

Brain teaser includes all the questions that cannot be classified into the previous categories we covered, but are often asked in the interview. This type of questions sometimes presents themselves as a probability question that requires brutal force enumeration of large number of combinations, or as a mathematic problem that needs extensive computation. However, if you are misled by the disguise, you will usually end up spending lots of time trying to solve the problem with diligent labor, without success. But if you believe that you are as smart as most of the other candidates, and you still can not solve the problem within the short interview time, say 20 minutes, then you should think about if you are going in the right direction or not. This section puts together a few typical brain teaser questions, just to give you a taste of how this kind of questions would look like. Try not to go with the first answer you come up with, and to think outside of the box to find the hidden gotcha behind the scene.

6.8.1 Horse Racing

Let's say you have 25 horses, from which you want to pick the fastest 3 horses. In each race, only 5 horses can run at the same time because there are only 5 tracks. What is the minimum number of races required to find the 3 fastest horses without using a stopwatch?

6.8.2 Trailing Zeros

Count the number of trailing 0s in $(100!)$. How about general $(n!)$? Note: $n! = 1 \times 2 \times \ldots \times n$.

6.8.3 Two Eggs Problem

You are in a 100 floor building, and you have 2 identical eggs. You can drop the egg from any floor. The egg will only break if it is dropped from floor T, or higher, and it will never break if it is dropped from floor lower than T. Now, given that you are allowed to break both the eggs, find the minimum number of drops to decide the value of T. How about in the worst case?

Chapter 7

Solutions to Technical Interview Questions

7.1 Probability Theory

7.1.1 Coin Flipping

If you keep throwing a fair coin, how many times on average do you need to flip to get two consecutive observations of the same side (both heads or both tails)?

Solution:
Let P_n be the probability that we get two consecutive observations at the first time after continuously throw a fair coin n times ($n \geq 2$). That is, the probability of observing HTHT...THH, THTH...HTT. Therefore, $P_n = \frac{1}{2^{n-1}}$. Then the expected number

of times

$$E[n] = \sum_{n=2}^{\infty} n P_n = \sum_{n=2}^{\infty} \frac{n}{2^{n-1}} = 3$$

7.1.2   Biased Coin

Given 10 coins with 1 biased coin and 9 fair coins. The biased coin has probability $p > 0.5$ to be head. Now randomly pick one coin and throw it three times. The observation sequence is head, head, and tail. What's the probability that the selected coin is the biased one?

Solution:
In this question, we need to compute the posterior probability of a biased coin given the observation sequence. There is only one biased coin out of ten coins. We have the prior probability of a biased coin $\Pr(biased) = 0.1$. The selected coin is thrown three times independently. Thus we have the conditional independency

$$\Pr(HHT|biased) = \Pr(H|biased)\Pr(H|biased)\Pr(T|biased).$$

Using Bayes' rule we have,

$$
\begin{aligned}
\Pr(biased|HHT) &= \frac{\Pr(HHT|biased)\Pr(biased)}{\Pr(HHT)} \\
&= \frac{\Pr(H|biased)\Pr(H|biased)\Pr(T|biased)\Pr(biased)}{\Pr(HHT|biased)\Pr(biased) + \Pr(HHT|fair)\Pr(fair)} \\
&= \frac{p^2(1-p) \times 0.1}{p^2(1-p) \times 0.1 + (1-p)^2 p \times 0.9} \\
&= \frac{0.1 \times p}{0.1 \times p + 0.9 \times (1-p)}
\end{aligned}
$$

7.1.3   Fair Result from a Biased Coin

Suppose you are given a biased coin, which has probability $p > 0.5$ to be head. How can you use this biased coin to get a fair coin toss. More specifically, how do you use this biased coin to generate a sequence of heads and tails in which the probability of getting a head is the same as the probability of getting a tail.

Solution:
This is a tricky question. Candidates need to understand the difference between conditional probability and marginal probability well to answer this question. We know that we only have a bias coin with $\Pr(head) = p > 0.5$. This is the marginal probability of getting a head. The question of designing a way to get a fair coin toss result is equivalent to finding an event such that the conditional probability of getting a head given that event is neural, i.e., $\Pr(head|event) = 0.5$. We only have a coin so the result from each toss is independent. Thus when we toss the coin twice, the probability of getting a head first then a tail is the same as the probability of getting a tail first then a head. The order of head won't matter, as the tosses are independent. Therefore, the event we are looking for will be the result subsequent toss is different from the current one. Formally, we have

$$\Pr(X_1 = head | X_1 \neq X_2) = 0.5,$$

where X_1 and X_2 are random variables for the results of the first and second coin toss, respectively. Based on the above analysis, we can derive a way to get fail coin toss result from a bias coin:

1. Toss the coin twice

2. If the results are the same, start over and go to step 1

3. If the results are different, output the result of the first toss and discard the result from the second one.

In this way, we can get a sequence of fail coin toss results from a biased coin.

7.1.4   Dice Payout

You are allowed to roll a dice at most three times. You will receive x dollars reward where x is the highest roll you get. You can choose to stop rolling at any time. For example, you get a six on you first roll then you can stop. What is the expected payout?

Solution:
The payout doesn't change if we don't stop after you roll a six on the first or second run, since the reward is the maximum roll. Let X be the maximum of three rolls. $X = 1$ if we always roll 1. $X \leq 2$ if we only roll one or two for each roll. $X \leq 3$ if we only roll one, two, or three for each roll. By applying the same reasoning, we have:

$$
\begin{aligned}
\Pr(X = 1) &= (\frac{1}{6})^3 \\
\Pr(X = 2) &= (\frac{2}{6})^3 - \Pr(X = 1) \\
\Pr(X = 3) &= (\frac{3}{6})^3 - \Pr(X = 1) - \Pr(X = 2) \\
\Pr(X = 4) &= (\frac{4}{6})^3 - \sum_{i=1}^{3} \Pr(X = i) \\
\Pr(X = 5) &= (\frac{5}{6})^3 - \sum_{i=1}^{3} \Pr(X = i) \\
\Pr(X = 6) &= 1 - (\frac{5}{6})^3
\end{aligned}
$$

Finally, we can compute

$$E[X] = \sum_{i=1}^{6} i \times \Pr(X = i) = 4.96$$

7.1.5 Finding Tesla

During the lunchtime suppose you are sitting by the street, you find that there is 64% chance observing at least one Tesla in one hour. What is the probability that you observe at least one Tesla in half an hour?

Solution:
There is 36% chance $(1 - 0.64 = 0.36)$ that there is no Tesla passing by in one hour, which means there is no Tesla in the first half hour and there in no Tesla in the second half hour. Then, the probability that no Tesla in half an hour is 60% since $(0.6 * 0.6 = 0.36)$. We can conclude that the probability of observing at least one Tesla in half an hour is 40%.

7.1.6 Mark Balls

There are 100 balls, numbered from #1 to #100. Each ball has its number marked on it. Now let's define a process P as: randomly choose a ball, if the ball already has a star on it, put it back, otherwise mark the ball with a star and then put it back.

1. After repeating the process P for 100 times, find the ball that is marked with number #1. What is the probability that the ball doesn't have a star on it?

2. What is the number of times that you need to repeat this process P, if you want to get all the balls marked with star.

Solution:
1) This question involves knowledge of geometric distribution, which represents the probability distribution of the number X of independent and identically distributed Bernoulli trials needed to get one success. Each time, the probability of picking ball K is $1/100$, for any K from 1 to 100. Hence, the probability of ball K not being picked in each process is $(1 - 1/100)$. Now, since each process is conducted independently, the probability of ball K not being picked in all 100 processes is $(1 - 1/100)^{100} = 0.366$.

2) This problem is also known as the coupon collector problem. Let X be the number of times needed in order to collect all $N = 100$ distinct balls, and let X_k be how many more times we need to pick a new ball once our collection contains $k - 1$ distinct balls (the total number of times may get quite large, with many repeats of the same balls). Clearly $X_1 = 1$. On each pick, the probability of collecting a new ball, given that we already have $k - 1$ different balls, is $p_k = (N - k + 1)/N$. That is, X_k follows a geometric distribution and

$$E(X_k) = 1/N_K = \frac{N}{N - k + 1}.$$

Note that this means when we've collected $N - 1$ different balls, we expect to still have to repeat N more times before getting that last ball needed! The total expected number needed is then

$$E[X] = \sum_{i=1}^{N} E[X_i] = \frac{N}{N} + \frac{N}{N-1} + \ldots = \frac{N}{1} = \lceil N \log N \rceil.$$

When $N = 100$, then we have

$$E[X] = \lceil 100 \log 100 \rceil = 461.$$

7.1.7 Playoff Games

Say there are two teams, A and B. The probability A wins is p. The series ends after 4 games if one team wins all four games. What is the probability of 7-game series? What p maximizes the probability of 7-game series?

Solution:
In order for the series to end in 7 games one team must win exactly 3 out of the first 6 games (in any order) and then win the seventh game. Therefore the probability is

$$\Pr(7 \text{ games}) = C(6,3)p^3(1-p)^3 = 20 \times p^3(1-p)^3.$$

Take the derivative with respect to p, we have

$$\frac{d(\Pr(7 \text{ games}))}{dp} = 60p^2(1-p)^3 - 60p^3(1-p)^2.$$

Set the derivative to zero we have $p = 0.5$.

7.1.8 Rolling A Four

What is the probability of rolling a 4 with 2 dice? What's the probability of rolling at least one 4 out of 2 dice.

Solution:
Let (a, b) denote a possible outcome of rolling the two die, with

a the number on the top of the first die and *b* the number on the top of the second die. Each of a and b can be any of the integers from 1 through 6. There are 36 possibilities for (a,b). [(1,3), (2,2), (3,1)] are all the ways a first die and second die add up to 4. The probability = 3/36 = 1/12.

For the probability of rolling at least one 4 out of 2 dice, we have combinations with the forms (4,x), (x,4), (4,4), with x in (1,2,3,5,6). There are 11 ways in total. The probability = 11 / 36.

7.1.9   Broken Computers

Your department has 20 computers and 4 of them are broken. If we randomly sample 12 computers from those 20 (without replacement), what is the probability of getting at least 3 broken computers?

Solution:
There are $\binom{12}{20}$ number of ways to sample 12 desktops from 20 computers. The probability of getting at least 3 broken computers is the sum of 1) the probability of getting exactly three broken computers and 2) the probability of getting all four computers. For 1), we are getting exactly three broken computers and the rest are good computers. The number of ways to sample three computers from four broken ones is $\binom{3}{4}$, and to sample 9 good computers from 16 good ones is $\binom{9}{16}$.

Similarly, the number of ways to get 4 broken computers are $\binom{4}{4}$. The total probability of sampling 12 computers from 20 without replacement and at least 3 are

$$\frac{\binom{3}{4} \times \binom{9}{16} + \binom{4}{4} \times \binom{8}{16}}{\binom{12}{20}}$$

7.1.10 Ant Collisions

Three ants are sitting at the three corners of an equilateral triangle. Each ant randomly picks a direction and starts to move along the edge of the triangle. What is the probability that none of the ants collide? Follow-up: k ants are sitting at the k corners of an equilateral polygon. Each ant randomly picks a direction and starts to move along the edge of the polygon. What's the probability that none of the ants collide?

Solution:
The ants can only avoid a collision if they all decide to move in the same direction (either clockwise or anti-clockwise). If the ants do not pick the same direction as others, for instance, if two ants move clockwise and one moves anti-clockwise, there will definitely be a collision. Each ant has the option to either move clockwise or anti-clockwise, with equal probability. There is a one in two chance that an ant decides to pick a particular direction. Therefore,

$$
\begin{aligned}
\Pr(\text{ No collision }) \quad=\quad & \Pr(\text{ All ants clockwise }) \\
+\quad & \Pr(\text{ All ants counter-clockwise }) \\
=\quad & 1/2 * 1/2 * 1/2 + 1/2 * 1/2 * 1/2 \\
=\quad & 1/4.
\end{aligned}
$$

More generally, for k ants,

$$
\begin{aligned}
\Pr(\text{ No collision }) \quad=\quad & \Pr(\text{All ants clockwise }) \\
+\quad & \Pr(\text{ All ants counter-clockwise }) \\
=\quad & 1/2^k + 1/2^k = 1/2^{k-1}
\end{aligned}
$$

7.1.11 American Family

Let X be the number of children in an ordinary American family. Let $\Pr(X = i) = p_i$, for $i = 1, 2, 3, 4$, and $\Pr(X > 4) = 0$, what is the probability that there are at least two girls in a family?

Solution:
Assuming the gender of each baby is identical independent distributed (i.i.d.), with probability being a girl q. Let Y be the number of girls in a family:

$$
\begin{aligned}
\Pr(Y >= 2) &= \sum_{j=2}^{4} \Pr(Y = j) \\
&= \sum_{j=2}^{4} \sum_{i=j}^{4} \Pr(Y = j | X = i) \Pr(X = i) \\
&= q^2 * p_2 + 3 * q^2 (1 - q) * p_3 + 6q^2 (1 - q)^2 p_4 \\
&+ q^3 * p_3 + 4q^3 (1 - q) * p_4 \\
&+ q^4 * p_4 \\
&= q^2 * p_2 + (3q^2 - 2q^3) * p_3 \\
&+ (6q^2 - 8q^3 + 3q^4) * p_4,
\end{aligned}
$$

when $q = 1/2$, we have $\Pr(Y >= 2) = \frac{1}{4} p_2 + \frac{1}{2} p_3 + \frac{11}{16} p_4$

7.2 Statistical Inference

7.2.1 Disease Diagnosis

You're testing for a rare disease, with 1% of the population is infected. You have a highly sensitive and specific test: 99% of sick patients test positive, and 99% of healthy patients test negative. Given that a patient tests positive, what is the probability that the patient is actually sick?

Solution:
The prior probability of sickness is Pr(sick) = 0.01. Since 99% of sick patients are tested positive, we have Pr(positive | sick) = 0.99. And 99% of healthy patients are tested negative, indicating Pr(positive | not sick) = 0.01. Using Bayes' rule we have the posterior probability that the patient is actually sick given a positive test result:

$$\Pr(\text{sick} \mid \text{positive}) = \Pr(\text{sick}) \frac{\Pr(\text{ positive } \mid \text{ sick })}{\Pr(\text{positive})},$$

where the marginal probability

$$
\begin{aligned}
\Pr(\text{positive}) &= \Pr(\text{ positive } \mid \text{ sick }) \Pr(\text{sick}) \\
&+ \Pr(\text{ positive } \mid \text{ not sick }) \Pr(\text{not sick}) \\
&= 0.0099 + 0.0099
\end{aligned}
$$

Finally we have

$$\Pr(\text{sick} \mid \text{positive}) = 0.5$$

7.2.2 Maximize Click Through Rate

Assume you are about to start an email campaign about your company's latest product. You can choose to send out emails to potential customers at anytime, for instance, 6am, 2pm, and 11pm. When to send emails to users so that you can get maximum click through rate (CTR)?

Solution:
Click through rate (CTR) is a very common metric to measure the success of many online applications and are being used in almost every Internet companies. It is a metric that measures the extent to which the presented content is relevant or interesting to the customers, and measures the effectiveness of engaging customers. Some typical applications of using CTR include measuring the success of a piece of online advertisement, of a website feature, or of links sent through email campaigns. CTR is usually defined as the number of users clicking a specific link in a webpage or an email divided by total customers this link is shown. The granularity of CTR can be defined by time, e.g., CTR per day.

When answering this type of problem solving and modeling questions, we encourage the candidates to start from the simplest model and assumption and engage in a conversation with interviewers. The complexity of model and assumptions can be increased step by step, depending on the feedbacks from the interviewers.

The simplest model
The simplest model is to send out emails at the same time of the day for all customers. We want to find a certain hour of the day which yield the maximum clicks across all customers. The formulation of this assumption is: $t = \underset{t}{\arg\max} f(t)$, where t can belong to each of the 24 hours during the day and $f(t)$ means the total number of clicks. A simple way to calculate t is for every hour in a day, average its clicks on all email on campaigns across a recent period of days. The hour with the highest number is the time we want to send out emails.

Adding more time factors in the model

Usually customer online behaviors, such as purchases, browsing, clicks and impressions are influenced by time, i.e. hour of the day, day of the week, week of the month, and month of the year. For example the problem can become: $t = \operatorname*{argmax}_t f(t, \text{day of week})$. t can be calculated as the same way in previous section. For example tomorrow is Wednesday and we want to send out our email campaign. We can collect all previous Wednesday click data of email campaigns and calculate which t yields the maximum clicks across all customers. Similarly we can also consider week of month, month of year etc. But we need additional analysis to see if those two time factors affect click through rate. Introducing these two factors can make data sparser with higher variance.

Maximize the probability of clicks for individual customers

In previous models, if we just take the hour with the maximum CTR, we have assumed an unrealistic distribution of CTR that peaks at that hour. This assumption can be easily invalidated by looking at the histogram of the number of CTR per hour. We will find out besides the peak hours there are other hours there are plenty of Clicks too. In other words, the time of clicks varies by customers and even to the extent of how relevant this email content to the users.

To build a more accurate model which takes customers and content into consideration, we can do a better job at estimating $\Pr(\text{Click} \mid \text{time, customer features, content features})$. When we decide to send an email to a customer, we can calculate $\Pr(\text{Click} \mid \text{time, customer features, content features})$ for all hours and choose the largest Pr.

For simplicity we can first assume a linear combination of time, customer, content features can give a reasonable estimation of $\Pr(\text{Click} \mid \text{time, customer features, content}$

features).

Use regression model to estimate the probability of clicks

Now the problem becomes how we estimate Pr (Click | time, customer features, content features). We can use a regression model by fitting the model to historical data. Logistic regression is preferred over linear regression here is because linear regression can yield an arbitrary real number. Instead estimating the probability of whether a user will click or not is more appropriate in this context. Also one can consider probit regression. Probit regression differs from logistic regression in that it assumes a normal distribution of errors, where logistic regression assumes a standard logit distribution. Which one to choose really depends on how well each model fits the data.

Improve the regression model

To further improve the prediction of clicks, one can do a bit of feature engineering to get the right feature from customer and content. We can also add more time features assuming e.g. day of week, month of year will also affect an individual customer's response to emails. However when adding more features we need to be careful that we have enough training data to avoid the over fitting issue.

Another important trick to improve the prediction is to factoring in the prior of clicks, or Pr (Click). In reality one can go through the historical data and find generally clicks are very few, e.g. around 1%. That means we can only get very rare positive signals. One practical way to factor in the prior is to do stratified sampling, or heavily downsampling the negative data points. But downsampling your data set essentially introduce bias to your model, you have to adjust your model after training. For example, if you are building a logistic regression model to predict the clicks as we described above, you will have to adjust the intercept,

β_0, from your down sampled regression according to the formula from Hosmer and Lemeshow, 2000:

$$\beta_c = \beta_0 - \log \frac{p_+}{1 - p_+}$$

where p_+ is the faction of positive cases in your pre down sampling population.

7.2.3 Is This Coin Unfair?

Given a coin you don't know it's fair or unfair. Throw it 6 times and get 1 tail and 5 head. Determine whether it's fair or not. What's your confidence value?

Solution:
To tell whether a coin is fair can be formulated as a statistical hypothesis test. The null hypothesis is the coin is fair. The alternative hypothesis is the coin is not fair.

Assume the random variable X is 1 when getting tail and 0 when getting head. X follows a Bernoulli distribution i.e. $X \sim B(p)$, where p is the expected value of probability of getting a tail.

Therefore the null hypothesis becomes $p = 0.5$. The sample size is relatively small we can choose t statistic as the effective size.

In our observation, the sample mean μ is $\frac{1}{6}$. The sample variance can be calculated as:

$$\frac{1}{n-1} \sum_{i=1}^{n} (x_i - \mu).$$

The variance is therefore $\frac{1}{6}$. The t statistics is

$$\frac{\frac{1}{6} - 0.5}{\frac{\sqrt{(\frac{1}{6})}}{\sqrt{(6)}}} = -2.$$

We can use the absolute value 2 as the reported t statistics.

Besides a t statistics, one also needs a confidence interval value to decide whether this t statistics are significant to reject the null hypothesis. Or formally speaking, we need to compare -2 to the confidence interval of mean estimation. The $(1 - \alpha)\%$ confidence interval can be calculated:

$$(\bar{X} - t_{1-\frac{\alpha}{2},5}, \bar{X} + t_{1-\frac{\alpha}{2},5}),$$

where $t_{1-\frac{\alpha}{2},5}$ is the t distribution critical value for a two sided test with $(1 - \alpha)\%$ and degree of freedom 5. For one sample t test the degree of freedom is simply the sample size minus 1.

If we choose $\alpha = 0.1$, we can look up a t distribution critical value table and the value of $t_{0.95,5}$ is 2.0150, the confidence interval is $(\frac{1}{6} - 2.0150, \frac{1}{6} + 2.0150)$. The value -2 falls out of the confidence interval so we can reject the null hypothesis and say the coin is unfair.

If we choose $\alpha = 0.05$, the value of $t_{0.975,5}$ is 2.5706, thus the value -2 lies within the confidence interval so we can not reject null hypothesis and we can not conclude whether the coin is fair or not.

7.2.4   Yes, It Is Raining

You're about to get on a plane to Seattle. You want to know if you should bring an umbrella. You call 3 random friends of yours who live there and ask each independently if it's raining.

Each of your friends has a 2/3 chance of telling you the truth and a 1/3 chance of messing with you by lying. All 3 friends tell you that "Yes" it is raining. What is the probability that it's actually raining in Seattle?

Solution:

In order to resolve this problem, first you should get to know what is the prior probability p that it's raining on any given day in Seattle. Since it is not mentioned in problem description, you should ask your interviewer. For instance, in this case let's assume that $p = 25\%$. Then apply Bayes' rule to compute the posterior probability of raining giving the information that all 3 friends tell you that "Yes".

Since the answers are independent:

$$
\begin{aligned}
\text{Pr(Yes,Yes,Yes | Raining)} &= \text{Pr(Yes | Raining)}^3 \\
\text{Pr(raining | Yes,Yes,Yes)} &= \text{Prior(raining)} \\
&\times \text{Pr(Yes,Yes,Yes | Raining)} \\
&/ \text{Pr(Yes, Yes, Yes)} \\
\text{Pr(Yes,Yes,Yes)} &= \text{Pr(Raining)} \\
&\times \text{Pr(Yes,Yes,Yes | Raining)} \\
&+ \text{Pr(not-Raining)} \\
&\times \text{Pr(Yes,Yes,Yes | not-Raining)} \\
&= 0.25 * (2/3)^3 + 0.75 * (1/3)^3 \\
&= 0.25 * (8/27) + 0.75 * (1/27) \\
\text{Pr(Raining | Yes,Yes,Yes)} &= 0.25 * (8/27) \\
&/ (0.25 * 8/27 + 0.75 * 1/27) \\
&= 8/11
\end{aligned}
$$

7.3   Dataset Manipulation

7.3.1   Consecutive Number

Assume a MySQL table "logs" with columns timestamp and jobID. The table log contains information about the history of job failures. Find all the jobIDs that appear at least twice consecutively. Please answer in a single query and assume read-only access to the database (i.e. do not use CREATE TABLE).

Table Names: logs	
Column Name	Data type
timestamp	Integer
jobID	Integer

For example, given the table:

timestamp	jobID
1	1
2	2
3	1
4	1
5	3
6	2
7	1
8	4

The only jobID that appears twice consecutively is 1. Once you answer this question, the interviewer might extend the question to arbitrary k: find all jobIDs that appear at least k times consecutively.

Solution:

The naive solution is doing a self join, which consumes $\mathcal{O}(n^2)$ time for a table with n rows.

CODE 7.1: Consecutive Number Self JOIN

```
1  SELECT
2      DISTINCT a.jobID
3  FROM
4      logs a,
5      logs b
6  WHERE
7      b.timestamp = a.timestamp + 1
8      AND a.jobID = b.jobID
```

Alternatively, we can maintain two variables to indicate how many times a jobID has appeared consecutively. It takes $\mathcal{O}(n)$ time.

CODE 7.2: Consecutive Number Local Variable

```
1  SELECT   DISTINCT(jobID)
2  FROM (
3      SELECT
4      jobID,
5      @counter := IF(@prev = jobID, @counter + 1, 1) ↩
            AS cnt,
6      @prev := jobID
7      FROM Logs y, (SELECT @counter:=1, @prev:=NULL) ↩
            tmp
8  ) counts
9  WHERE cnt >= 2
```

7.3.2 Music Actions

Assume we have a PostgreSQL database. Given two tables music_action and summary_table.

- Summarize that, for each client, how many pieces of music (including duplicate ones) do they listen to so far?

- Write a function to update the summary_table using the music_action table with the latest snapshotDay.

Please answer in a single query and assume read only access to the database (i.e. do not use CREATE TABLE).

The music_action is a table recording daily music listened by clients.

Table Names: music_action	
Column Name	Data type
actionID	Integer
clientID	Integer
musicID	Integer
snapshotDay	Timestamp

and the summary_table is:

Table Names: summary_table	
Column Name	Data type
clientID	Integer
numPlay	Integer
musicID	Integer
endDate	Timestamp

The summary_table is an accumulative table, which means each row is the number of times each clientID listened to musicID up to endDate.

Solution:
The question tests your knowledge about GROUP BY and dif-

ferent types of JOIN. Especially for the second question, simply joining the summary_table with the music_action will remove all the rows in summary_table that is not in music_action with the latest snapshot day. Use LEFT OUTER JOIN instead.

CODE 7.3: Music Actions

```
1  -- Summarized for each client, how many music do ←
       they listen
2  SELECT
3      clientID,
4      COUNT(actionID) as numPlay
5  FROM music_action
6  GROUP BY clientID
7
8  -- Update latest day new music_action to ←
       summary_table
9  WITH new_client_music_summary AS (
10 SELECT
11     clientID AS clientID,
12     musicID AS musicID,
13     COUNT(actionID) AS counts,
14     MAX(snapshotDay) AS endDate
15 FROM music_action
16 GROUP BY
17     clientID,
18     musicID
19 )
20
21 SELECT
22     M.clientID,
23     (M.counts + S.numPlay) AS numPlay,
24     M.musicID,
25     CASE
26         WHEN (S.endDate IS NULL or S.endDate < M.←
               endDate)
27         THEN  M.endDate
28         ELSE S.endDate
29     END as endDate
30 FROM new_client_music_summary M
31 LEFT OUTER JOIN summary_table S
32    ON S.clientID = M.clientID
```

```
33    AND S.musicID = M.musicID
```

7.3.3 No Sales

Create three tables a) *accounts*, which contains accountid
b) *dates*, which contains dateid c) *facts*, which contains three
columns date, accountid and revenue. The facts table records the
expense of an account every day if there is expense. If there is no
expense then there won't be a record in the facts table. Given this
scenario write a SQL query that generates a list of all Accounts
on every day in the last 30 days that had no expense.

Solution:
The solution query:

CODE 7.4: No Sales

```
1   CREATE TABLE accounts (
2       accountid BIGINT
3   );
4
5   CREATE TABLE dates (
6       dateid DATE
7   );
8
9   CREATE TABLE facts (
10      accountid BIGINT,
11      dateid DATE,
12      revenue NUMERIC
13  );
14
15  SELECT
16      d.dateid,
17      a.accountid
18  FROM
19      accounts a
20  CROSS JOIN dates d
21  LEFT OUTER JOIN (
```

```
22   SELECT
23       DISTINCT f.accountid, d.dateid AS dateid
24   FROM facts f CROSS JOIN dates d
25   WHERE (d.dateid - f.dateid) <= 30
26   AND (d.dateid - f.dateid) >= 0
27   ) active ON
28       a.accountid = active.accountid
29       AND d.dateid = active.dateid
30   WHERE
31       active.dateid is NULL
```

7.3.4   Second Highest Sale

Assume we have a PostgreSQL database, and a table Sales, which is a table with product and sales information. Write a SQL query to find out the second highest sale from the Sales table. Please answer in a single query and assume read-only access to the database (i.e. do not use CREATE TABLE).

Table Names: Sales	
Column Name	Data type
productID	Integer
sale	Numeric

If there is no second highest salary, then the query should return NULL. Once this problem is solved, interviewer will most likely increase the difficulty level by either moving to get the Kth sale or asking to write queries without some database specific built-in features like TOP, LIMIT, or ROW_NUMBER.

Solution:

We can start with using the LIMIT clause in MySQL, whose syntax is like: *LIMIT offset, count*. The offset defines how many rows are going to remove from the results; for example, the offset of the first row is 0, not 1. The count defines maximum number of rows to return. When there is only one argument after $LIMIT$, this argument will be used to specifies *count* where $offset = 0$.

CODE 7.5: Second Highest Sale using LIMIT

```
1    SELECT sale FROM sales ORDER BY sale DESC LIMIT 1 ↩
         OFFSET 1
```

You can change *offset* argument to $N - 1$ if the question is extended to highest N-1 sale. If we are asked to take away the built-in feature LIMIT, we can create a subquery by removing the max sale in the table then select the max sale from the resulting view.

CODE 7.6: Second Highest Sale using IN

```
1    SELECT
2        MAX(sale) AS second_highest_sale
3    FROM sales
4    WHERE sale NOT IN (
5        SELECT MAX(sale)
6        FROM sales)
```

Instead of using IN clause, we can use '<' operator.

CODE 7.7: Second Highest Sale using <

```
1    SELECT
2        MAX(sale) AS second_highest_sale
3    FROM sales
4    WHERE sale < (
5        SELECT MAX(sale)
6        FROM sales)
```

If the interviewer extends this question and asks you to find the k-th highest sale, you can write the so-called correlated subquery, where the inner query or subquery references outer query. Replace '2' in the below query with any k the interviewer asked.

CODE 7.8: Second Highest Sale Correlated subquery

```
1  SELECT DISTINCT sale
2  FROM sales s
3  WHERE 2 = (
4      SELECT COUNT(DISTINCT sale)
5      FROM sales s2
6      WHERE s.sale <= s2.sale
7  )
```

We can also use special keyword LIMIT in Postgres (also MySQL) to find the second, third or Nth highest sale, together with using ORDER BY clause to sort the rows first. We fist find the highest k sales in the subquery using ORDER BY DESC and return the lowest row by using ORDER BY.

CODE 7.9: Second Highest Sale using LIMIT

```
1  SELECT sale
2  FROM (
3      SELECT DISTINCT sale
4      FROM sales
5      ORDER BY sale DESC
6      LIMIT 2
7  ) AS s
8  ORDER BY sale
9  LIMIT 1
```

7.3.5   TF–IDF

Given a corpus table with columns pageid, text, for example, all Wikipedia documents keyed by pageid, write HIVE/MYSQL queries to calculate the tfidf of each word.

Solution:

Given a corpus table named corpus with columns pageid (type BIGINT) and text (type STRING). To calculate TF-IDF, we need to prepare a relation consists of (pageid, word), compute the term and document frequency, and finally calculate the tf–idf value.

CODE 7.10: TF–IDF

```
1   CREATE OR REPLACE VIEW corpus_exploded AS
2   SELECT
3       pageid,
4       word
5   FROM
6       corpus LATERAL VIEW explode(tokenize(text, true))↩
            t as word;
7
8   CREATE OR REPLACE VIEW tf AS
9   SELECT
10      pageid,
11      word,
12      COUNT(word) AS freq
13  FROM corpus_exploded
14  GROUP BY pageid, word
15
16  CREATE OR REPLACE VIEW df AS
17  SELECT
18      word,
19      COUNT(DISTINCT pageid) ndoc
20  FROM
21      corpus_exploded
22  GROUP BY words;
23
24  select count(distinct pageid) from corpus;
25  set hivevar:n_docs=10000000;
26
27  SELECT
28      tf.pageid,
29      tf.word,
30      ( 1 + LOG(CAST(tf.freq AS FLOAT)) )
31              * LOG(CAST({n_docs} AS FLOAT) / df.ndoc) ↩
```

```
                   AS tfidf
32  FROM tf
33  JOIN df ON
34     tf.word = df.word
35     AND df.ndoc > 1
36  ORDER BY tfidf desc;
```

7.3.6 Top K Sales

Assume a PostgreSQL database. Given schema Sales, which is a table with product and sales information. Write executable SQL queries to find out top 3 products for each category in terms of sales on a daily basis. Please answer in a single query and assume read-only access to the database (i.e. do not use CREATE TABLE).

Table Names: Sales	
Column Name	Data type
ProductID	Integer
ProductName	CHAR(50)
Sales	Numeric
SalesDate	Date
Category	CHAR(20)

Solution:

The interviewee needs to clarify with interviewer what exactly "top 3" means and how to deal with ties. For example, if product A has 100 sales, B has 100 sales, C has 100 sales, D has 90 sales, and E has 89 sales. Does " top3" mean A,B,C or A,B,C,D,E? Also are the ProductID unique among all products?

The query below assumes returning top 3 products in each category purely based on sorting their daily sales numbers and product ID is unique:

CODE 7.11: TOP K Products

```
1   WITH R AS (
2   SELECT
3       Category,
4       ProductID,
5       ProductName,
6       SalesDate,
7       Sales,
8       ROW_NUMBER() OVER (PARTITION BY Category, ←
            SalesDate ORDER BY sales desc) AS Sales_Rank
9   FROM product_sales
10  )
11  SELECT
12      S.Category,
13      S.SalesDate,
14      S.ProductID,
15      S.ProductName,
16       R.Sales_Rank,
17      R.Sales
18  FROM product_sales S INNER JOIN R
19  ON
20      S.ProductID = R.ProductID
21      AND S.SalesDate = R.SalesDate
22  WHERE R.Sales_Rank <= 3
23  ORDER BY S.Category, S.SalesDate, R.Sales_Rank
```

But this query has a problem when there are more than 3 products have tie in sales. Only 3 products among them will be returned. A better way is to get top products with top 3 distinct sales numbers, change the **ROW_NUMBER()** to **DENSE_-RANK()**. **DENSE_RANK()** essentially generates the same rank number when the Sales number is the same.

7.4 Product, Metrics and Analytics

7.4.1 New Messenger App

An Internet company recently enforced users to use a standalone Messenger App and deprecated the chat functionality on the company's mobile App. To track the performance of this move, what metrics will you use?

Solution:
In this case, we analyze the metrics before and after launching the stand alone messenger App. One consideration point when choosing the metrics is to look at the total metrics before and after the change, without delineating the impact on the Company's general purpose mobile App.

1. The number of daily active users and monthly active users are good indicators to see whether we lose users, or experience reduced activity by enforcing them to use a standalone Messenger App. We can compare the number of total users of both mobile App and messenger App after the change, with the number of users of the mobile App before the change. This metric should provide insight on whether the deprecation has significant impact on the App users.

2. The total time spent on the old integrated mobile App vs. the total time spent on the new App plus the total time spent on the standalone Messenger App.

3. The number of messages sent or received. Again, compare the metric between the standalone Messenger App and the old integrated mobile App.

4. The time taken for a user to send or respond a message. Compare the metric between the standalone Messenger App and the old integrated mobile App.

In some circumstances, even with an increased total time and active users on both new mobile App and the standalone Messenger App, we cannot simply claim that this is a good move. For example, the company does care about the advertisement revenue and the clicks generated from mobile App functions other than messenger. It is possible that after the change, the users spend most of their time on the standalone App, but they don't use the mobile App anymore. So a few more metrics need to be considered if there is also a business need to maintain the user engagement of the mobile App after the change:

1. Revenue generated by the general purpose mobile App before and after the change.

2. Click through rate or number of impressions of the general purpose mobile App excluding the ones generated from the chat functionality.

7.4.2   Incorrectly Implemented Search Algorithm

To test a new search relevance algorithm, we performed an A/B testing. The control group would see search results returned by original algorithm, while the treatment group would see search results returned by new algorithm. During the process of A/B testing, engineers realized that the new algorithm was not fully validated and it was not implemented correctly, which resulted in lower relevance in search results than the original one does. Due to this, the test was terminated. However, when data scientist looked at this A/B testing result, surprisingly, on average people in treatment group performed more search queries than people in control group. Meanwhile, the advertising revenue was higher in treatment group than in control group.

Question 1:
    How would you explain that the new algorithm results in

people performing more searches than the original algorithm?

Question 2:

How would you explain why the new algorithm generates more advertising revenue?

Question 3:

It looks like the incorrectly implemented new algorithm resulted in higher advertisement revenue. Would you recommend putting the new algorithm into production?

Solution:

This is a good example of how interview questions test candidates' product sense as well as understanding of metrics. To better elaborate on this question, one should have good understanding on A/B testing as well as metrics. If you want to know more about A/B test, please refer to Chapter 6.4 and 7.4. Please be aware that this type question is most likely to be open ended: there is not right and wrong answer. The explanation below demonstrates one way to answer it. However, this is not the only way. For instance, the answer listed below is base on the assumption that the A/B test is not set up correctly. One could also tackle this problem from validating how the test is been set up. Regardless which assumption you choose, keep your assumptions in mind, and be consistent when you answer follow-up questions.

Question 1:

Let's divide our users into two groups, patient ones and impatient ones. Since the new algorithm wasn't correctly implemented, the search results actually have lower relevance than before. It means that it's more difficult for users to find what they want during search. In the short term, the patient users' average search queries per session would increase, while the impatient users' would keep the same. This is because for patient users, they don't easily give up when the search doesn't return what they want. Instead, they would try to revise the query and search again within the same search engine. On the other hand, for the impatient users, no matter whether they get satisfied results or not, they are not going to search more queries per session. Thus for this group of people, search queries per session will be constant. Combine the effects from these two group of users, the overall search queries per session would go up.

Question 2:

Depending on how advertisement is served, we can have different scenarios why advertising revenue is going up. On the one hand, if the advertisement display was on a separate widget than the search results, and it didn't change when the search algorithm changed: assume users will always see the same ads. The more time the users spent on searching, the more exposure they would have to these ads. This can result in an increase of the click through rate of the advertisements. In this case, the increase in advertisement revenue is due to the longer time users stay on the site. On the other hand, if the advertisement was served as part of the search result, but had a separate algorithm from the search algorithm, then a worse search algorithm can make the advertisement look more relevant, in which case, the frustrated users are more likely to click on the advertisement for relevant information. In this case, the increase in advertisement revenue is due to the relative higher relevance of the advertisement to the user query than the standard search result.

Question 3:

My answer in this case is NO. The supporting arguments for moving to the new algorithm are that there are more search queries per session and more advertisement revenue. However, this does not show the whole picture. We need to think about both short term and long term effects of the action. The answers in Question 1 and 2 explained why the new algorithm increased search queries per session and advertisement revenue. In the short term, the customers may not easily change their habit and leave. However, it is also very unlikely that they will stay for long if search results don't improve. Therefore, keeping the buggy algorithm in production would eventually drive the revenue down.

Generally, if we want to put a new algorithm into production, first we need to develop criteria to figure out under what circumstance we will move to new algorithm, and select metrics correspondingly. In this case, the number of search queries per session is a good metric, but itself alone does not tell the whole story. Many other related metrics need to be taken into consideration. For instance below are some other important metrics:

- We need to know the number of Abandonments and Abandonment Rate. Abandonments measure the number of times when users perform some searches, and then go to other website, without clicking into search results. Abandonment Rate is calculated with the number of abandonments divided by the number of sessions. If the Abandonment Rate increases dramatically, it could imply that users are not finding what they need, so that they give up using this search engine for querying this particular content. It is possible that they move to another search engine instead. We need to consider both Abandonments as well as Abandonment Rate, since Abandonment Rate is also affected by the number of sessions.

- We also need to know the number of Active Users, to be more specific, daily active users. We could define the daily active users as users who perform search queries in a session day. Irrelevant search results tend to drive people away from this search engine. The marketplace for search engine is competitive; if one were not doing a good job, users would turn away to the competitors. In that case, there will be a drop in daily active users.

- The Click Through Rate is also vital. This rate reveals lots of information about whether the users find relevant web links and choose to click into them or not.

In summary, the two metrics mentioned in the Questions, search queries per session and advertising revenue, do not provide enough information to support the decision that we should implement the new algorithm in production. Actually, based on the analysis in Question 3, we should not bring the new algorithm in production.

7.4.3   Reduce Gas Efficiency

Assume Country M depends heavily on foreign oil. One of the major consumption comes from cars. There are two types of cars, A and B. The number of people in Country M who use A and B are the same. They drive similar distances each month. Good news comes that there are two new technologies, X and Y (of equal cost). If applying X, mpg (mile per gallon) of A would increase from 50 mpg to 75 mpg. If applying Y, mpg of B would increase from 10 mpg to 11 mpg. The goal is to decrease the gasoline consumption in order to reduce the dependency on importing foreign oil. At this moment, Country M could only afford one of the new technologies, either X or Y.

Question 1: As the consultant of the president, which technology would you recommend to use?

Question 2: After applying the technology of your choice, assuming there is more fund available for research on new technology, which car would you choose to conduct research for?

Solution:
Product questions usually involve a bit of context and requires candidates to formulate a problem to solve. Candidates are also expected to extract useful information in the question and use them as clues and evidence for problem solving. It is very common there is some information missing or unknown, candidates are expected to make valid assumptions and to unravel the problem step by step. During the process, we encourage candidates start with the simplest assumption and use concrete examples to walk through the problem solving process when ever possible.

Question 1. Back to this question, the goal here is to reduce the consumption of gasoline. Based on consumptions listed in the question, people who use type A car and people who use type B car drive similar distance each month.

We can make a simple assumption that the average commute distance per month is 1000 miles for them. If that were the case, type A car would consume 20 gallons while B would consume 100 gallons without adopting the new technologies.

It is straightforward to calculate that if applying X, A would consume 13.3 gallons, saving 6.7 gallons. B would keep constant. And if applying Y, B would consume 90.9 gallons, saving 9.1 gallons. A would keep constant. The following table shows the current gas consumption (in gallon) and the consumption if applying X and if applying Y, respectively.

Car Type	Current MPG	MPG w/ X	MPG w/ Y
A	20	13.33	20
B	100	100	90.91
Total	120	113.33	110.91

We can conclude that applying Y would result in more reduction in the gasoline consumption.

If the candidate wants to demonstrate his or her thoroughness in thinking and the capability to generalize the solution mathematically, we encourage the candidate to further check whether the above conclusion will apply in all data points. For example, now we assume average commute distance per month is D. When applying X, the change of type A car's consumption is $\frac{D}{50} - \frac{D}{75} = \frac{D}{150}$, there is no change in B car's consumption; when applying Y, the change of type B car's consumption is $\frac{D}{10} - \frac{D}{11} = \frac{D}{110}$. Because $\frac{D}{110}$ is always larger than $\frac{D}{150}$, applying Y will always result in more reduction in gasoline consumption under the assumption.

Question 2. This follow up question is open ended, we first need to understand the objectives of choosing investing into one technology over another. For example, we can say as a country we want to choose the cheaper technology given they reduce the same amount of gasoline consumption; we can also say as a country we want to maximize the reduction of gasoline consumption given investing same amount of money to each technology. Different objectives will formulate different problems.

In this question, for example, we will choose the cheaper technology among X and Y given they can reduce the same amount of gasoline consumption.

However the question did not provide the information how difficult to increase 1mpg for type A car or type B car, i.e. investing the same amount of money in to research, how much mpg type A car would increase and how much type B would increase. This will require the candidates to come up with a reasonable assumption to move forward on this question. For example we can start with a very simple assumption, when increasing 1 mpg for both cars, the research dollar costs on X and Y are the same.

Given the objectives and the assumption, we can formulate the question as comparing the dollars spent on researching car A technology to save x gallon and the dollars spent on researching car B technology to save x gallon. Assume we will need to increase y mpg (spending y dollars) for car A to save x gallon, the equation is:

$$\frac{1000}{100} - \frac{1000}{10 + y} = x$$

or equivalently:

$$y = \frac{1000}{100 - x} - 10$$

Similarly we will need to increase $y\prime$ mpg (Spending $y\prime$ dollars) for car B to save x gallon, the equation is:

$$y\prime = \frac{1000}{20 - x} - 50$$

We can plot y and $y\prime$ as a function of x, i.e. given saving same amount of gallon x, how y and $y\prime$ look like. Once we know our goal to save a specific number of x gallons, we can choose the technology corresponding to the lesser of y and $y\prime$.

We can also formulate the problem in a similar way if we use a different assumption, for example, the research dollar costs are the same to increase 1 percent mpg for both cars. It is less important which objectives or assumptions to use than letting the interviewers know your thinking process, your objectives and assumptions. It is also important for them to know that you are aware of the assumptions you make, what some other options are and the limitations of each assumptions if possible.

7.5 Experiment Design

7.5.1 The Power of a Statistical Test

What is the definition of power? What are some factors that affect the power of the test? How does the power of the test relate to p-value in a certain test?

Solution:
The power of a statistical test is the capability to detect that an effect actual exists. In this context it is the capability of detecting that the metrics of treatment is different from control, when it is truly the case. Probabilistically, the power of test is: Pr(reject null hypothesis | null hypothesis is false) It can also be expressed as $1 - \beta$, where β is Pr(fail to reject null hypothesis | null hypothesis is false). β is also usually termed as *Type II error*. Qualitatively speaking, here is the list of factors that could affect the power:

- Standardized effect size. It is value of the statistical test. For example in the simplest t test, the standardized effect size is t score: $\frac{\hat{x}-\mu}{S_x}$ where $\hat{x}$ is the sample mean, μ is the true mean, and S_x is the standard variations of the population. When standardized effect size increases, statistical power increases (positive relationship), holding other components constant. A large standardized effect size means that a sample statistic is substantially different from a hypothesized value; therefore, it becomes more likely to detect the effect.

- Variability or standard error.

- Type I error. Type I error is defined as Pr(reject null hypothesis | null hypothesis is true). It is often termed as α, or the significance level of a statistical test. Usually Type I error or the significance level is pre defined, e.g. 0.05 by convention. This sets the standard for how extreme the data must be before we can reject the hypothesis. If we carry out a less conservative test by increasing the Type I error to 0.1, we now can reject null hypothesis when the data is less extreme. In other words, we increase the chance the null hypothesis will be rejected. Considering the power of test is Pr(reject null hypothesis | null hypothesis is false), we are in fact in crease the power. Therefore when allowing a larger Type I error, we are increasing the power of the test

p-value is related to α. Once the α is set, a statistic e.g. t-statistics is computed. Each statistics has an associated probability value called p-value, or the likelihood of an observed statistic occurring due to chance, given the sampling distribution. In other words, p-value measures how extreme the data are. For example with a very small p-value ($\ll 0.0001$) we say there are 0.01% chance we observe this data is due by chance. Therefore we believe the data is indeed very extreme. By comparing p-value with Type I error we can decide if we are going to reject the null hypothesis.

If we sets a larger α we in fact allows a larger p-value to be considered significant, therefore increase the power of the test.

7.5.2   Sixty Four Designs

A website is testing its new designs of a page. They came up with 63 designs. Together with current design there are 64 different designs. They want to test all of them and choose the best. How will you set up the experiments, and calculate and report the results?

Solution:
There are multiple ways to answer this question.

t test among pairs of treatment

To start with, a simple solution can be running all those designs simultaneously. Assuming each treatment has enough samples to have the desired power, incoming customer sessions can be randomized and assigned to one of the 64 treatments. After running the experiment for a period of time, we stop and analyze the results by running a statistical test, e.g. t test, between each of the new designs against the control example, i.e. the current one.

p-value correction

Such an experiment which tests n dependent or independent hypotheses on a set of data is a multiple inference problem. With multiple hypotheses test we increased the likelihood of a rare event will be witnessed, or we increase the likelihood to reject a null hypothesis when it is actually true (or type I error). In the other word, we need a more stringent p value to determine what is significant. The most simple correction way is Bonferroni correction. It tests each individual hypothesis at a statistical significance level of $\frac{1}{n}$ times what it would be if only one hypothesis were tested. For example if we are testing 64 designs with a desired $\alpha = 0.05$, then the Bonferroni correction would test each individual hypothesis at

$$\alpha = \frac{0.05}{64} \doteq 0.00078$$

. For any website design with p value larger than this value they are insignificantly different than the current one. For those that show significant result, we can rank the magnitude of the statistics that being measured and pick the top one.

Adaptive experiment design

However in reality among the 64 designs, there can be some "bad" designs and others are very popular ones. We don't need wait until the end of the experiment to identify those obviously bad ones. By terminating bad designs early, we can stop bad impact on customers; we can re distribute samples into other on going treatments, therefore increase the power of testing those remaining treatments. This belongs to scope of adaptive experiment design.

What makes adaptive experiment design different from conventional A/B testing is some aspects of the experiment changes during the process. In this case treatment samples will change during the process. What makes adaptive experiment design trickier to report results is the p-value calculation. p-value is calculated based on a specific experiment design, if the design changes during the process, the p-value calculation should also change.

7.5.3   The Lovely New Feature

We want to add a new feature to our product. How to determine whether people like it or not?

Solution:
The general idea is to do an A/B testing.

First of all, some metrics need to be defined to measure whether this feature has met the business expectation, i.e. whether customers like it or not. Some useful metrics can be defined along the line of revenue, profit or the increased number of user engagement e.g. click through rate, impression rate, bounce rate etc.

Secondly, prepare two versions of your products, for instance, a website, with one version having the new feature, and the other one without. You should be able to simultaneously serving both of them to customers.

Thirdly, split your test population into a treatment group and a control group. Make sure such split did not introduce any bias. A common way to do this is Simple Random Sampling (SRS) 50% vs. 50%. There are multiple ways to define your test population. The split can be done at website session level. But sometimes if you care about the effect on individual customer and one customer can have multiple sessions, you can also split the population by customers by counting multiple sessions towards one customer. This is especially useful if you want to test your new features across multiple devices.

Finally, prepare the following elements as of a standard hypothesis testing:

- You need to define a null hypothesis for your hypothesis testing. The null hypothesis can be that the treatment metrics is not different from the control.

- Pre-define the Type I error you can tolerate in your weblab. In statistical hypothesis Type I error is Pr(reject null hypothesis | null hypothesis is true) or false positive rate. It is usually termed as α. With a pre-defined Type I error one can find the corresponding alpha depending on the statistical test chosen. i.e. Pr(reject null hypothesis | null hypothesis is true) = Pr(p value < α) = Type I error. Based on this one can judge based on the p value if the result is significant.

- Assess the power of your statistical tests. The power of statistical test is the capability to detect whether an effect actual exists. In this context it is the capability of detecting the metric of treatment is different than the control when it is truly the case. Or Pr(reject null hypothesis | null hypothesis is false). It can be also expressed as $1 - \beta$, where β is the Type II error.

There are also two practical considerations when running a

A/B test on a website:

- The running time of the campaign. Increase running time can get more samples and successfully fend off noise. However if the metrics drop it can bring real loss.

- Dealing with the outliers. There are two simple ways to deal with outliers. One way is to truncate at a certain percentile of metrics of the population, e.g. 99.9%. The other way is to visualize the outliers and have a hand picked threshold.

7.5.4   Your Samples Are Biased

How do you know if your sample is biased? What would you do if your sample is actually biased?

Solution:
If you know the true mean of your population, sample your samples multiple times to check if the mean of samples are normally distributed around the true mean.

If you do not know the true mean of your population, you can investigate if your sampling method and process has the following bias:

- Selection Bias: mistakenly exclude some part of the population.

- Measurement Bias: the method of measurement tends to generate observations that differ from the true value of the response. For example, when sampling from a time variant signal, if the sampling frequency is lower than the signal changing frequencies, the observed value of the signal is wrong.

- Non-response Bias: when the population we measured values for has systematically different response than the population we did not or could not measure values for. For example, we can measure the average TTL (time to live) of ping to understand the network traffic delay. TTL is a metric that measures how long it takes for a unit of data to be sent to and then came back from a point in the network. We cannot just use those servers that are responded. Those do not respond can have significantly longer TTL.

If you know an entire group of population has been excluded from the sampling process, then there is hardly any way to correct the estimate from the biased samples. However, if the sample bias just causes the over representativeness or under representativeness of one group, a simple way to correct sampling bias is to re-weight the data points. Suppose in true population there are 50% of group A and 50% group B, but after sampling there are 80% of group A and 20% group B, we can attach a weight 0.625 to samples in group A and 2.5 to samples in group B.

7.6 Coding

7.6.1 Binary Sequence Decoding

We use a sequence of 1 to encode a message. 11 represents a k, 1 represents a a. Suppose we receive a sequence of 1 with length N, how many different phrases can we decode?

Solution:
We could do it recursively. Let $C(N)$ be the number of decoding ways for length N. Apparently, $C(1) = 1$. $C(2) = 2$. For any N, the decoded phrases end either with k or with a. Since 11 encodes k, there are $C(N-2)$ different phrases ending with k. Likewise, there are $C(N-1)$ different phrases ending with a. Hence, we have $C(N) = C(N-1) + C(N-2)$, which is a *Fibonacci sequence* and has a closed form solution. To solve it numerically within linear time, the iterative approach is recommended.

CODE 7.12: Binary Sequence Decoding

```
1   def fib(n):
2       a, b = 1, 1
3       while n > 0:
4           a, b = b, a+b
5           n -= 1
6       return a
```

7.6.2 Majority Element

Given an array with size n, a *majority element* is an element that appears more than $\lceil n/2 \rceil$ times. Write a function that returns the majority element if it exists, otherwise returns None/NULL.

Solution:
The basic solution is to iterate through each element, and check if each element is a majority of the array, which takes $\mathcal{O}(n)$ time

to finish. The total complexity is then $\mathcal{O}(n^2)$.

A better solution is to sort the array first. If the majority exists, it has to be at index $\lceil n/2 \rceil$, whose value can then be checked if it's the majority element using $\mathcal{O}(n)$ time. This approach takes $\mathcal{O}(n \log n)$ in total.

An $\mathcal{O}(n)$ algorithm for this problem is known as Moore's Voting algorithm. The basic idea is that if the majority does exists, we can always find another value to pair with each instance of majority element we've seen so far and cancel this pair out. After we cancel out all non-majority element, the majority one will still exists. To see how this works, we can maintain two variables candidate and count. We first process the first element and assign the first element to candidate and 1 to count. For each following element, we increase the count by 1 if the element equals to candidate, and decrease the count by 1 otherwise. Whenever the count variable drop to zero at some point m, we can conclude that 1) m must be even, 2) we have consume at most $m/2$ majority elements and at least $m/2$ non-majority element. That means, we always have more majority elements than non-majority ones in the remaining array. Therefore, when count drops to zero, we set candidate be the next element and set count to be 1. When the iteration finishes processing the last element, we can make sure we have consumed all the non-majority elements and the candidate is the majority.

CODE 7.13: Majority Element

```
1  def majorityElement( num):
2      candidate = num[0]
3      count = 1
4      for j in range(1, len(num)):
5          if num[j] == candidate:
6              count += 1
7          else:
8              count -= 1
```

```
9              if count < 0:
10                  candidate = num[j]
11                  count = 1
12         if checkMajority(num, candidate):
13             return candidate
14         else:
15             return None
16
17   def checkMajority(num, candidate):
18       count = 0
19       for a in num:
20           count += 1 if a == candidate else -1
21       return count > 0
```

7.6.3 Pow(x, n)

Implement pow(x, n) where x is a double and n is an integer.

Solution:

This is a numerical computation problem. The naive approach is to compute the product of n copies of x, which takes $\mathcal{O}(n)$ time. But using the recursive equation $pow(x, n) = pow(x^2, n/2)$ we can reduce the integer by half after each iteration until the n becomes 0 where $x^0 = 1$. In this way we can have an $\mathcal{O}(\log(n))$ computation time. Note that n is integer, we need to handle corner cases such as 1) if n is negative then $pow(x, n) = pow(1.0/x, n)$, and 2) if n is odd. we have $pow(x, n) = pow(x, n - 1)$. Note that $\frac{n-1}{2}$ is an integer when n is odd.

CODE 7.14: pow

```
1   def pow(x, n):
2       if x == 0:
3           return 1
4       if x < 0:
5           return pow(1.0/x, -n)
```

```
6        if  x  %  2  ==  1:
7              return  pow(x,  n  -1)
8        else:
9              return  pow(x*x,  n/2)
```

7.6.4 Remove Element

Given an array and a target value, remove all instances that equal to target value and return the new length. This should be done in place. The order of elements can be changed. It doesn't matter what you leave beyond the new length.

For example, given an array $\{1, 2, 3, 2, 5\}$ and a target value 2. Your program should return 3 and modify the array such that the first 3 elements of the array are not 2.

Solution:

We can use the so-called two pointer technique to tackle this problem. We maintain two indexes, the first iterate through the array and the second one represents that any element of the array on its left doesn't equal to target.

CODE 7.15: Remove Element

```
1  def  removeElement(self,  A,  elem):
2        newLen  =  0
3        for  a  in  A:
4              if  a  !=  elem:
5                    A[newLen]  =  elem
6                    newLen  +=  1
7        return  newLen
```

7.6.5 Running Median

Given a stream of integers, return the median of numbers every time a new number is added. For example, integers coming in the following order: $[4, 6, 1, 3, 2, 0]$, then the function will return $[4, 4, 4, 3, 3, 2]$.

Solution:
The naive solution will sort the data as new integer arrives, then it's easy to get the median element. To insert a new element to a sorted array so that the new array is also sorted, the insertion sort algorithm can be used. If the integers are stored as an array, it takes $\mathcal{O}(\log(n))$ time to find where to insert the new element to the sorted array and $\mathcal{O}(n)$ time to move the following elements. If the integers are stored as a linked list, it takes $\mathcal{O}(\log(n))$ to find the right position for insertion. The total run time complexity of the function is then $\mathcal{O}(n^2)$ for a stream of n integers.

Alternatively, we can use the *heap* data structure. We store integers less than the running median in a max heap while integers greater than the running median are stored in a min heap. Upon arrival of a new integer, we maintain an invariant that the number of elements in both heaps differs at most by one element. The total run time complexity is then $\mathcal{O}(n \log(n))$

CODE 7.16: Running Median

```
1   def medianII(nums):
2       minHeap = []
3       maxHeap = []
4       soln = []
5       for n in nums:
6           if len(minHeap) == 0 or n >= minHeap[0]:
7               heapq.heappush(minHeap, n)
8           else:
9               heapq.heappush(maxHeap, -n)
10
11          if len(minHeap) > len(maxHeap) + 1:
```

```
12            topMin = heapq.heappop(minHeap)
13            heapq.heappush(maxHeap, -topMin)
14        elif len(maxHeap) > len(minHeap):
15            topMax = heapq.heappop(maxHeap)
16            heapq.heappush(minHeap, -topMax)
17
18        if len(minHeap) > len(maxHeap):
19            soln.append(minHeap[0])
20        else:
21            soln.append(-maxHeap[0])
22    return soln
```

7.6.6   Stock Prices

Given an array storing the historical prices of a stock where the ith element of the array represents the stock price at the ith hour, design an algorithm to find when to buy and sell one share of the stock to achieve the maximum profit. You are allowed to complete one transaction at most.

Follow up, what's the maximum profit you get if at most k transactions are allowed. k can be $2, 3, \ldots$ up to the number of elements of the array.

Solution:
To get the maximum profit, we want to buy as low as we can and sell as high as we can. We scan each element i of the array from left to right, and find out the maximum profit p_i we can possible get if we sell at i, which is the price at i minus the minimum price we observe so far. The maximum profit is then the maximum of

p_i.

CODE 7.17: Stock Prices

```
1   def maxProfit(prices):
2       if len(prices) <= 1:
3           return [0 0]
4       bestSell = 0
5       bestBuy = 0
6       maxProfit = 0
7       buy = 0 # prices[buy] will be the minimum price
8       for i in range(1, len(prices)):
9           curProfit = prices[i] - minPrice
10          if curProfit > maxProfit:
11              maxProfit = curProfit
12              bestSell = i
13              bestBuy = buy
14          if prices[i] < prices[buy]:
15              buy = i
16      return [bestBuy, bestSell]
```

To solve the follow-up question, we need to take a dynamic programming approach. On a given data j, we need to keep track of two variables. The first variable local is the maximum profit one can get with at most k transactions if the last transaction ends today. The second one global is the maximum profit one can get up to day j with at most k transactions.

CODE 7.18: Stock Prices with at most K transactions

```
1   def maxProfit(k, prices):
2       if len(prices) == 0:
3           return 0
4       # Effectively infinite transactions
5       if k > len(prices):
6           maxProfit = 0
7           for i in range(1, len(prices)):
8               diff = prices[i] - prices[i-1]
9               maxProfit += max(diff, 0)
10          return maxProfit
```

```
11
12      local = [0 for j in range(k+1)]
13      profit = [0 for j in range(k+1)]
14      for i in range(1, len(prices)):
15          diff = prices[i] - prices[i-1]
16          for j in range(k, 0, -1):
17              local[j] = max(local[j] + diff,
18                             profit[j-1] + max(diff, ↩
                               0))
19              profit[j] = max(local[j], profit[j])
20      return profit[k]
```

7.6.7 Two Sum

Given an array of integers, and a target T. Find two numbers in the array such that the sum equals to T. The function twoSum takes inputs of an array of integers and a target value; return the indices of two numbers, where index1 must be less than index2. You may assume that each input have exactly one solution. What if the input array is sorted?

Solution:
We can maintain a map which maps the value of the element in the array to its index. When we encounter an element, we can look up the map using the key equal to target minus the value of the element. If we can find it in the map, we can find the indices in the array whose values sum up to target. The run time complexity is $\mathcal{O}(n)$, and the memory is $\mathcal{O}(n)$.

CODE 7.19: Two Sum

```
1   def twoSum(self, num, target):
2       mappings = {}
3       for i in range(len(num)):
4           mappings[num[i]] = i
5       for i in range(len(num)) and mappings[val] != i:
6           val = target - num[i]
```

```
7            if val in mappings:
8                 return [i, mappings[val]]
9         return [-1,-1]
```

When the array is sorted, we can employ the so-called two-pointers method.

CODE 7.20: Two Sum Sorted

```
1  def twoSumSorted(self, num, target):
2      l = 0
3      r = len(num) - 1
4      while l < r:
5          s = num[l] + num[r]
6          if s == target:
7              return (l, r)
8          elif s < target:
9              l += 1
10         else:
11             r -= 1
12     return (l, r)
```

7.6.8 CTR Estimation Using Map-Reduce

You are asked to compute the click through rate (CTR) for advertisement from a large number of page logs. Each page log contains information such as ad_id (Integer type), is_shown (boolean type), and is_click (boolean type). How to compute the CTR for each ad as well as the overall CRT, using the map-reduce framework.

Solution:
Map-reduce is a distributed computational framework where each mapper processes one piece of the input data and generates a pair of key and value. The generated pairs of key and value from mappers are aggregated by reducers in such a way that the

reducers perform a summary operation over all values of the same key generated by mappers.

CODE 7.21: CTR Map Reduce

```
1   def mapper(key = None, value = log):
2       if log.is_shown:
3           yield (log.ad_id, log.is_click)
4           # use key = -1 to summarize overall CTR
5           yield (-1, log.is_click)
6
7   def reducer(key, value_iterator):
8       clicks = 0
9       counts = 0
10      while value_iterator.has_next():
11          click = value_iterator.next()
12          clicks += click
13          counts += 1
14      yield (key, 1.0 * clicks / counts)
```

7.7   Machine Learning

7.7.1   Decision Tree

Answer the following questions regarding to the decision tree model.

1. How does decision tree decide the splitting criteria? Can we use decision tree for regression? What are the splitting criteria for decision tree regression?

2. When a feature X in the data set is a continuous random variable with probability density function $p(x)$, which is a Gaussian distribution with mean μ and variance σ^2, please derive its entropy $H(X)$. Name one property of the entropy you derived above that doesn't hold for any discrete random variable.

3. What are the advantages of decision trees?

4. If one of the features has very high cardinality (the number of values), how will it affect the decision tree model building process?

5. What are the main differences between boosting trees and random forests?

6. Write a simple program to generate a decision tree given X, XValues and Y. X is a $N \times D$ matrix of training features where each row is an example and each column is a feature. The values of each feature are comparable and have only limited number of distinct values. XValues is a $D \times V$ matrix for all distinct feature values. Each row represents all possible distinct values of a feature. Y is an $N \times 1$ vector of labels. Suppose there already exists a function to compute the information gain.

Solution:
This question covers the basis properties of a decision tree.

1. Decision tree can rely on information gain to decide the splitting criteria. Other criteria includes Gini's index which based on impurity and variance reduction. Yes, we can also use square loss as the splitting criteria. For a data set with supervised signal Y, we can define the square loss as $\sum_{i=1}^{N}(Y_i - \bar{Y})^2$ where $\bar{Y} = \sum_{i=1}^{N} Y_i / N$.

2.

$$
\begin{aligned}
H(x) &= -\int p(x) \log p(x) dx \\
&= -\int p(x)(-\frac{\log(2\pi\sigma^2)}{2} - \frac{(x-\mu)^2}{2\sigma^2}) dx \\
&= \frac{\log(2\pi\sigma^2)}{2} + \frac{1}{2\sigma^2} \int p(x)(x-\mu)^2 dx \\
&= \frac{\log(2\pi\sigma^2) + 1}{2}
\end{aligned}
$$

When $\sigma^2 < \frac{1}{2\pi e}$, we have $H(x) < 0$. Note that the entropy for discrete variable is always non-negative.

3. Some of the advantages of decision trees are:

   a) Decision tree models are easy to understand and interpret.

   b) Decision tree applies on heterogeneous features (numerical, categorical etc.).

   c) No feature normalization is needed.

   d) Prediction with decision tree is generally very fast.

4. When the cardinality of a feature is very high, the decision tree algorithm tries to split the value in every possible way to compute the information gain. Therefore it slows the tree model building process.

5. Boosting trees algorithms reassign weights to different samples based on the classification results from previous iterations. In terms of data set, Random forests applies bootstrap aggregation (bagging) to train different trees, where different subsets of data are sampled and used to train different model. Boosting tree algorithms are iterative algorithms where the execution of current iteration is based on the results from the previous one. Random forests can be easier to deploy on distributed systems since each tree in random forest can be trained independently.

6. Assuming the features values are comparable and have only limited distinct values, the algorithm of a decision tree in python is:

CODE 7.22: Decision Tree

```
1   class DecisionTree:
2       def __init__(self):
3           # When splitFeature == -1, it becomes a↵
                leaf node
4           # with splitValue the score of this ↵
                leaf.
5           self.splitFeature = -1
6           self.splitValue = -1
7           self.left = None
8           self.right = None
9           self.gainThr = 1.0e-3 # for example
10
11      def growATree(self, X, XValues, Y):
12          N = len(X)
13          numFeatures = len(X[0])
14          maxGain = self.gainThr
15
16          for i in range(numFeatures):
17              for val in XValues[i]:
18                  gain = self.entropyGain(X, XValues,↵
                        Y, i, val)
19                  if gain > maxGain:
20                      maxGain = gain
```

```
21                    self.splitValue = val
22                    self.splitFeature = i
23       if splitFeature == -1:
24           return self.splitValue = entropy(Y)
25
26       leftX = []
27       rightX = []
28       leftY = []
29       rightY = []
30       for j in range(N):
31           if X[j][splitFeature] <= splitValue:
32               leftX.append(X[j][:])
33               leftY.append(Y[j])
34           else:
35               rightX.append(X[j][:])
36               rightY.append(Y[j])
37       self.left = self.growATree(leftX,
38                                  XValues,
39                                  leftY)
40       self.right = self.growATree(rightX,
41                                   Xvalues,
42                                   rightY)
```

7.7.2 Linear Regression

What is the basic assumption of using a linear regression? How do you empirically access that your distribution is normal? What are the most common estimation techniques for linear regression?

Solution:
Linear regression models the relationship between dependent variable y and independent variable x.

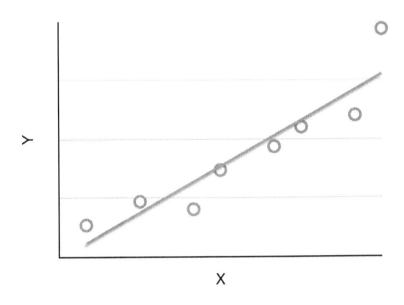

The two main assumptions of using a linear regression are:

1. The relationship between the dependent variable y and the explanatory variables X is linear.

2. The residual errors from regression fit are normally distributed.

We can normalize a distribution and use QQ plot against normalized Gaussian distribution to empirically assess whether a distribution is normal. Most estimation methods include ordinary least squares (errors are homoscedastic) and generalized least squares (errors are heteroscedastic). Penalized version of the least squares loss functions such as, L2 norm penalty (ridge regression) and L1 norm penalty (Lasso), are usually used to fit the linear regression models.

7.7.3 Logistic Regression

What's formula for logistic regression? How to determine the coefficients given the data?

Solution:
The logistic function

$$\delta(t) = \frac{1}{1+e^{-t}}$$

t is a linear function of the feature vector (explanatory variables) x.

$$t = \beta_0 + \beta_1 x$$

And the logistic function can be written as

$$F(x) = \frac{1}{1+e^{-(\beta_0 + \beta_1 x)}}$$

$F(x)$ can also be interpreted as the probability of the data point being the positive class. The coefficients are estimated with maximum likelihood estimation (MLE) [1].

The candidates are encouraged to use the principal of MLE to work through the mathematics of estimating coefficients of logistic regression, because being able to do the derivations rather than just naming a concept will demonstrate your thorough understanding of this concept and will impress interviewers.

7.7.4 Multi-class Logistic Regression

Assume that we have K different labels and each data point x has d dimensional features. By conversion, capitalized letters represent random variables, and lower case letters represent the

---

[1] http://en.wikipedia.org/wiki/Maximum_likelihood

value of the random variable. The posterior probability for label k is then:

$$\Pr[Y = k | X = x] = \frac{\exp(W_k^T x)}{1 + \sum_{i=1}^{K-1} \exp(W_i^T x)}$$

for $k = 1, \ldots, K - 1$.

1. How many parameters do we need to estimate? What are these parameters?

2. Given n training samples $X \in \{x_1, \ldots, x_l, \ldots, x_n\}$ and $\{y_1, \ldots, y_l, \ldots, y_n\}$, please write down explicitly the log likelihood function.

3. Compute the gradient of L with respect to each w_k and simplify it.

4. Add the L^2 regularization term $\frac{\lambda}{2} \sum_i ||w_i||^2$, compute the gradient of the new cost function f.

Solution: 1. There are $(K - 1) \times d$ parameters.

2. Let the vector $W = (w_1, \ldots, w_{k-1})$.

$$\begin{aligned} L(w_1, \ldots, w_{K-1}) &= \sum_{l=1}^{n} \log \Pr[y_l | x_l] \\ &= \sum_{l} \log \frac{\exp(w_{y_l}^T x_l)}{1 + \sum_i \exp(W_i^T x_l)} \\ &= \sum_{l} [w_{y_l}^T x_l - \log(1 + \sum_i \exp(w_i^T x_l))] \end{aligned}$$

3.

$$\nabla L(w_k) = \sum_{l} [I(y_l = k) - P(y = k | X = x_l)] x_l$$

4.

$$\nabla f(w_k) = \nabla L(w_k) - \lambda w_k$$

7.7.5 Naive Bayes

1. Given the training data (X, y), what assumptions do the Naive Bayes methods make?

2. Suppose X is a vector of n boolean features and y is a discrete variable with m possible values, let $\theta_{ij} = P(X_i | y = y_j)$. What's the number of independent θ_{ij} parameters. Now suppose X is a vector of n continuous features and $P(X_i = x_i | y = y_j) \sim N(x_i | \mu_{ij}, \sigma_{ij})$. How many distinct μ_{ij}, σ_{ij} are there?

3. Write maximum likelihood estimator (MLE) estimator for θ_{ij}.

Solution:

Naive Bayes is one of Bayesian classifiers which predict Y by modeling the probability $P(X|y)$.

1. Naive Bayes classifier assumes features of X are conditional independent of each other given Y.

2. For boolean features, the number of independent parameters is nm. For continuous features, there are nm distinct pairs of μ_{ij} and σ_{ij}

3. Let X_i^l denote the i-th feature of X of the l-th example in the training data, $l = 1, \ldots, L$. L is the number training examples.

   For boolean features, we typical model $P(X|y)$ with a Bernoulli distribution:

   $$P(X = X_i^l | \theta_{ij}) = \theta_{ij}^{X_i^l} (1 - \theta_{ij})^{1 - X_i^l}.$$

The likelihood can be written:

$$
\begin{aligned}
L(\theta_{ij}) &= \prod_{l=1}^{L} P(X = X_i^l | \theta_{ij})^{I(y^l = y_j)} \log L(\theta_{ij}) \\
&= \sum_l I(y^l = y_j)[x_i^l \log \theta_{ij} + (1 - x_i^l) \log(1 - \theta_{ij})]
\end{aligned}
$$

taking derivative with respect to θ_{ij} and setting 0:

$$
\frac{\partial \log L(\theta_{ij})}{\partial \theta_{ij}} = \sum_l I(y^l = y_j)[\frac{x_i^l}{\theta_{ij}} + \frac{1 - x_i^l}{1 - \theta_{ij}}] = 0
$$

we have

$$
\hat{\theta}_{ij} = \frac{\sum_l I(Y^l = y_j) x_i^l}{\sum_l I(Y^l = y_j)}
$$

7.7.6 Neural Network

Suppose there is a neural network with two input units X_1 and X_2, two hidden units h_1 and h_2, and an output unit o_1. The weights between X_1 and the two hidden units are w_1 and w_3, the weights between X_2 and the hidden units are w_4 and w_2. The weights between the output unit and hidden units are w_5 and w_6. There is no bias term in those units.

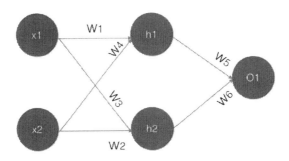

1. Suppose this network uses only linear activation functions. That is, the output of a unit is a linear combination of its inputs, weighted by the weights. For example, $h_1 = w_1 X_1 + w_4 X_2$. Redesign the network without any hidden units to compute the same function.

2. Is it possible to combine a multi-layered (deep) neural network with linear activation function into a single layer one without any hidden layer?

3. The activation of the neuron can be arbitrary. Suppose in our network, the activation function for the hidden units is the sigmoid function, which is $\frac{1}{1+\exp(-\sum_i w_i x_i)}$. The output of the output neuron, however, returns 1 only if the sum of the inputs from hidden units is greater than 0. Find the weights of this network so that it can output X_1 XOR X_2 where X_1 and X_2 are binary.

Solution:
Given the network defined in the problem, we have

1. Since the output $o_1 = w_5 h_1 + w_6 h_2 = (w_5 w_1 + w_3 w_6) x_1 + (w_4 w_5 + w_2 w_6) x_2$, we can connect X_1 with the output unit with a weight $w_1 w_5 + w_3 w_6$, and connect X_2 with the output unit with a weight $w_4 w_5 + w_2 w_6$.

2. Yes. Each layer performs a matrix multiplication and a network with multiple layers computes a chain of matrix multiplications. So we can represent the weights between input and output units as the product of weights across different layers.

3. Note that here, the activation function of the neurons is sigmoid. We can express XOR as: $(X_1$ XOR $X_2) = (X_1$ OR $X_2)$ AND NOT $(X_1$ AND $X_2)$. One possible solution is $w_1 = w_4 = 1, w_2 = w_3 = 10, w_5 = -6, w_6 = 5$. Then we have:

X_1	X_2	h_1	h_2	o_1
0	1	0.73	1	1
1	0	0.73	1	1
0	0	0.5	0.5	0
1	1	0.88	1	0

7.7.7 Overfitting

What are some of the issues you encounter when training machine learning models? What's overfitting? Have you ever overfitted your data? What causes overfitting? How to overcome overfitting?

Solution:
In model training process, overfitting may be an issue when the model does not generalize well on the trend in the data, but instead describing the random errors or noise. Overfitting is often caused by the over complexity of the model compared to the training data size. For example, if you data is in two dimensions, and you have five points in the training set, but the model is ten degree polynomial, it is likely to overfit the data. The overfitted model memorizes and tailors to the particularities of the training data. And when predicting the unseen data, it tends to perform poorly.

To avoid overfitting, you can try the methods below:

1. Increase the training data size. Providing *enough* data so that the underlying trend of the data can be captured. Increasing training data set can generally alleviate overfitting.

2. Split the data into mutually exclusive sets: training and test. Build model on the training set and evaluate performance on test set. Further you can use k-fold cross validation to optimize your model. K-fold cross validation is splitting

the data into k folds and hold one fold for testing and the rest for training, k times.

3. Regularization. The regularization term aims at measuring the model complexity. Regularization punishes over complex models.

4. Early stopping. In some iterative method such as gradient descent, you can apply early stopping to avoid over complex model.

5. Pruning. In decision tree, you can prune sections of the tree that does not provide much class-discrimination power with pruning techniques.

7.7.8 Regression Evaluation

How do you evaluate regression? In an online item click tracking system. We would like to predict the item click through rate (CTR). Some actual and predicted is shown in the table below:

ID	Actual CTR	Predicted CTR
1	005	0.06
2	0.69	0.78
3	0.22	0.19
4	0.58	0.57
...	...	...

How would you calculate the CTR prediction performance?

Solution:
Regression model evaluation metrics includes:

1. Explained variance score

$\hat{y}$ is the estimated target output and y is the actual target output. The explained variance is

$$\text{explained\_variance}(y, \hat{y}) = 1 - \frac{Var\{y - \hat{y}\}}{Var\{y\}}$$

2. Mean absolute error

$$\text{MAE}(y, \hat{y}) = \frac{1}{n} \sum_{i=1}^{n} |y_i - \hat{y}_i|$$

3. Mean squared error

$$\text{MSE}(y, \hat{y}) = \frac{1}{n} \sum_{i=1}^{n} (y_i - \hat{y}_i)^2$$

4. Coefficient of determination (R^2)

$$1 - \frac{\sum_{i=1}^{n} (y_i - \hat{y}_i)^2}{\sum_{i=1}^{n} (y_i - \bar{y}_i)^2}$$

in which

$$\bar{y} = \frac{1}{n} \sum_{i=1}^{n} y_i$$

The most popular one is arguably R^2 which is the ratio of the explained variance to the total variance. Therefore the ad CTR predicting results can be evaluated by, for example, calculating R^2. The closer it is to 1, the more correlated is between the actual value and the predicted value.

7.7.9 Support Vector Machine

1. What is a support vector machine?

2. What are the support vectors?

3. What differentiates it from other linear classifiers, such as the Linear Perceptron, Linear Discriminant Analysis, or Logistic Regression?

4. Describe three kernel functions and when to use which of them.

Solution:
The figure below shows how SVM finds a hyperplane that separates positive and negative examples by maximizing the so-called margin. For separable data sets such as the ones show in the figure, there are many possible linear decision hyperplanes. A reasonable choice would be the line that is in the middle of the void space between data points of the two classes.

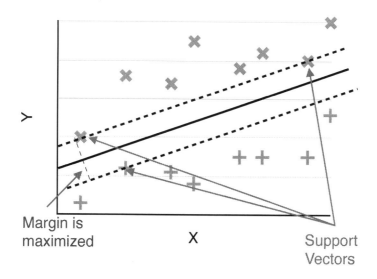

Margin is
maximized   X   Support
                                                    Vectors

1. Support Vector Machines formulate supervised machine learning problems as an quadratic programming problem. They are attempting to find a hyperplane that divides two classes with the largest margin.

2. The support vectors are the points right up against the margin of the decision hyperplane. Support vector machines focus on the points that are the most difficult to tell apart, in the contrary, other classifiers try to separate all of the points.

3. In addition to performing linear classification, the fundamental difference between SVMs and other linear classifiers is that SVM can efficiently perform nonlinear classification by using the so called kernel trick, which implicitly maps the linear non-separable inputs into high dimensional features spaces where inputs become linear separable.

4. In the absence of expert knowledge and assuming the problem requiring non linear models, the Radial Basis Function kernel is a good default one. When the number of examples is very large, one may just use the linear kernel. When the inputs are text, string kernels that measure the similarity between two strings work the best.

7.8 Brain Teasers

7.8.1 Horse Racing

Let's say you have 25 horses, from which you want to pick the fastest 3 horses. In each race, only 5 horses can run at the same time because there are only 5 tracks. What is the minimum number of races required to find the 3 fastest horses without using a stopwatch?

Solution:
Denote the 25 horses as H1, H2, ..., H25. Without loss of generality, we can conduct the below five races and assume the results to be:

- Race 1: H1 > H2 > H3 > ~~H4~~ > ~~H5~~

- Race 2: H6 > H7 > H8 > ~~H9~~ > ~~H10~~

- Race 3: H11 > H12 > H13 > ~~H14~~ > ~~H15~~

- Race 4: H16 > H17 > H18 > ~~H19~~ > ~~H20~~

- Race 5: H21 > H22 > H23 > ~~H24~~ > ~~H25~~

Now that we have eliminated 10 horses. The next game will be to decide the rank between the fastest horses of the previous 5 races. Again, without loss of generality, we can assume the result to be:

- Race 6: H1 > H6 > H11 > ~~H16~~ > ~~H21~~

In the sixth race, we eliminated the ~~H16~~ and ~~H21~~, as they are slower than at least 3 horses (H1, H6, H11). We can also eliminate the ones that are slower than them, namely, ~~H17, H18, H22, H23~~. With further examination, we can also eliminate the ~~H8~~ (slower than H1, H6, H7), and ~~H12, H13~~ (slower than H1, H6, H11). Now, we have H1, H2, H3, H6, H7, H11 left, among which we know H1 is the fastest. We just need to have the 7th game to determine the 2nd and 3rd places:

- Race 7: H2, H3, H6, H7, H11

Based on the results of Game 7, we can determine the fastest 3 horses.

7.8.2   Trailing Zeros

Count the number of trailing 0s in $(100!)$. How about general $(n!)$? Note: $n! = 1 \times 2 \times \ldots \times n$.

Solution:
The naive solution is to first compute $100!$, then count the number of trailing zeros.

Without actually computing $100!$, we can analyze which factors in $100!$ will produce a trailing 0. First, each multiplier of 10 will generate one 0. Since $2 * 5 = 10$, $12 * 15 = 180, \ldots$. We can conclude that any multiplier of5 will generate one 0. Moreover, $4 * 25 = 100$, $50 * 8 = 400$, $75 * 16 = 1200$, and 100, each will generate two 0 (or one extra 0 since each is a multiplier of 5). The answer is then $20 + 4 = 24$.

For solutions to general $n!$. A trailing zero is always produced by prime factors 5 (the number of 2s in prime factors is always more than or equal to the number of 5s). If we can count the number of 5s in its prime factor, our task is done. For example, $n = 5$,

$$5! = 2 * 3 * 2^2 * 5 = 2^3 * 3 * 5^1.$$

$n = 11$,

$$11! = 2^8 * 3^4 * 5^2 * 7.$$

There are always more 2 than 5 in the prime factors of $n!$. This simply computes

$$[n/5] + [n/5^2] + [n/5^3] + [n/5^4] + \ldots$$

and stops when the divisor gets larger than n.

CODE 7.23: Trailing Zeros

```
1  def zeroes(n):
2      i = 1
3      result = 0
4      while n >= i:
5          i *= 5
6          result += n/i
7      return result
```

7.8.3 Two Eggs Problem

You are in a 100 floor building, and you have 2 identical eggs. You can drop the egg from any floor. The egg will only break if it is dropped from floor T, or higher, and it will never break if it is dropped from floor lower than T. Now, given that you are allowed to break both the eggs, find the minimum number of drops to decide the value of T. How about in the worst case?

Solution:

There are different ways to find the value of T. However the question asks for the one with minimum number of drops. Let's start with the easiest solution

- Approach 1: try lowest floor first, and then go up one by one, namely, 1, 2, 3, ... T

This approach will need T drops, yet it uses only one egg. In the worst case, it will require *100* drops. A more efficient approach would be to use both the eggs. Hence we have the below solution.

- Approach 2: try lowest even floor first, then go up two by two, namely, 2, 4, 6, ... If the first egg breaks at floor 2K, try the second egg at floor 2K-1.

Further analysis tells us that this method needs at most $\lceil T/2 \rceil + 1$ drops. In the worst case, it would take *51* drops, when the first egg breaks at floor 100. It is easy to see that we can generalize the second method to jump D floor at once.

- Approach D: try floor D first, then go up to 2D, 3D, until the first egg breaks at K^{th} trial. Then we start from $D \times (K - 1) + 1$, go up one floor each time, until the second egg breaks.

This approaches would take at most $\lceil 100/D \rceil + D - 1$ drops. We take the derivative of

$$f(D) = 100/D + D - 1$$

wit respect to D and we get

$$f'(D) = -100/D^2 + 1.$$

Let $f'(D) = 0$, we have the best value of D to minimize it would be 10, in which case, the worst case would require *19* drops, when the first egg breaks at floor 100.

If we think one step further, the number of drops depends on the number of drops until you break the first egg, and the number of drops after that until you break the second egg. What if we can make the sum of these two numbers always equal, that would control the worst case drops. Here is the final solution:

- Approach D': try floor D first, then go up D-1 more floors, then D-2 more floors, until the first egg breaks at K^{th} trial. Then we start from the floor

$$D + (D - 1) + \ldots + (D - (K - 2)) + 1,$$

go up one floor each time, until the second egg breaks.

It is easy to see that this approach would take at most $k + D - k = D$ drops, as long as D is big enough for us to keep process going, meaning the step size doesn't reduce to 0 before we reach 100 floor. We have the best value for D would be the one that satisfies:

$$D + (D - 1) + (D - 2) + \ldots + 1 = \frac{D(D+1)}{2} \geq 100,$$

which gives $D \geq 14$. In the worst case, it would take 14 drops.

Made in the USA
San Bernardino, CA
26 September 2016